GATEWAY TO ITALIAN DICTION

A Guide for Singers

John Glenn Paton

D1616478

Cover photo: A gate to the Borghese Gardens, Rome.
Photo by John Glenn Paton.

Now a public park, the gardens are on land acquired during
the 1600s by Cardinal Scipione Borghese. Near this gate
is the Villa Borghese, a palatial structure that was not a
residence, but an art gallery and a center for festivities.
The Villa now houses an important collection of paintings,
as well as sculptures by Gian Lorenzo Bernini.

Table of Contents

Preface

Diction, a Gateway to Artistic Singing

The goal of Gateway books is to help singers achieve artistic communication and make an impact on their audiences through beautiful diction. Mastery of diction, always consistent with the finest vocal technique, is the key to expressiveness and vocal color. It is our responsibility to our audiences, as well as to the great poets and composers who created the music we love.

The premise of Gateway books is to consider diction always in relation to meaning, both poetic and musical. Every example, word or phrase is translated. The student never has to practice lists of meaningless words. Furthermore, every basic sound is presented in a musical phrase that can be sung immediately and then studied in the complete song found in the companion Gateway song anthology. Most example words come from lyric texts.

Learning diction poses an apparent dilemma: Individual sounds must be practiced in words, and practicing words require knowing other individual sounds. It seems as if one must learn everything at once. To accommodate various styles of learning, Gateway books present sounds in a simple and logical order that can be adapted flexibly. One can change the order of the chapters, learning about consonants before vowels, for instance, or vowels before syllabication. One may focus on the simpler sounds first or zero in on the problem sounds first, according to the strategy one prefers. Every possible Italian spelling can be located through the alphabetical index.

Since *Gateway to German Diction* was written, there is a new *Handbook of the International Phonetic Association*, presenting many revisions in terminology. It seemed important to adopt the new terms, even at the price of inconsistency with the German diction text already published, so that students who want to study further in phonetics and linguistics will be familiar with the scientific standard. I have kept some older terms that seemed more congenial to singers, and the difference is noted. To enrich our appreciation of the target language, Chapters 2 and 3 offer background material about its history and characteristics. Some well-known songs for group singing are also offered.

Packaged with this book is a supplementary CD that contains all of the example words spoken by a native Italian speaker. Exercise materials and worksheets are also available separately, with permission to reproduce them for classroom use.

Acknowledgments

Prof. Luigi Marzola, coordinator of the voice faculty of the Conservatorio di Musica "G. Verdi," Milan, read this book in detail and offered his comments generously and enthusiastically while we worked together at the computer. His clearly articulated concepts were completely in accord with principles learned earlier from my work with Signora Enza Ferrari, another superb vocal coach. I have also borrowed useful ideas that were freely offered by: Leslie De'Ath, Wilfred Laurier University, Waterloo, Ontario; Alessandro Manuali, Rome; Prof. Stuart Patterson, Conservatoire Nationale de Musique, Paris; Dr. Anna Siragusa and Dr. Salvatore Siragusa, Milan; Dr. Paolo Zedda, Université de Lyon. First-hand information about Neapolitan dialect came from Claudio Giova, Naples. Of course, none of the above persons is responsible for whatever errors this book contains.

My ideas and my ways of expressing them have been shaped by the students in 30 years of classes at the University of Colorado at Boulder and the University of Southern California. And the whole book has been meticulously edited by Joan Thompson, my wife, who insists on clarity and more clarity. I thank all of these colleagues warmly, as well as the skilled and imaginative persons who produce my books at Alfred Music.

John Glenn Paton
Los Angeles, California

Part I: Introduction

Chapter 1: Phonetic Concepts

To sing well in Italian is a vital part of a classical singer's training, opening a gateway into a rich repertoire of songs and to the passionate world of opera. Because Italian is not our native language, learning to sing it well requires conscious control of many details of pronunciation that come automatically to native speakers. If we aim to sound like Italians, we have to know and understand what we are doing much better than a native does. That is why we need to learn certain concepts and vocabulary that are not needed for speaking our mother tongue.

The following text explains basic concepts and traces connections between them. If some are not clear to you at the first reading, they will become clear as your work progresses. Each essential new term is printed in SMALL CAPITALS when it is introduced for the first time and defined, making it easy to find for later review.

Diction

DICTION means, for singers, the art of making the texts we sing clear to our listeners.

PRONUNCIATION involves choosing the best, most correct sound of a word, the one that is used by educated speakers and verified by dictionaries.

ARTICULATION means forming the sound correctly and efficiently with a minimum of physical tension. The lips, teeth, tongue and soft palate are articulators.

And the concept of diction has to include EXPRESSION, because emotional communication with our audience is the most important reason why we sing.

Phonetics

PHONETICS[1], the science of speech sounds, provides a great deal of useful information for singers. PHONETICIANS, the scholars of phonetics, are trained to analyze the sounds of any language, even a language that has never been written.

In analyzing languages, phoneticians use the INTERNATIONAL PHONETIC ALPHABET (IPA). In the IPA, one written symbol, and only one, stands for each speech sound in a language, regardless of how that language is written. The complete IPA contains both letters from our alphabet and symbols borrowed from other languages. It also includes additional markings called DIACRITICS that can be added to the symbols to account for small adjustments, such as a particular individual's tongue position. The IPA contains enough symbols to record any speech sound that a human being could possibly produce. A chart of the complete IPA, containing far more symbols than we need for European languages, is found on page 119.

PHONEMES are speech sounds that are significant to meaning. Every language uses only a selection from among the speech sounds that are humanly possible. In order to identify which phonemes a particular language uses, phoneticians study MINIMAL PAIRS, words whose meanings are only distinguished by the difference of a single phoneme.

Here is how such a study works: In English, "ten - den" is a minimal pair, two words that sound the same except for their initial consonants. Since the words have different meanings, /t/ and /d/ must be separate phonemes.

On the other hand, we might hear two persons say the word "no," one with only oral resonance and the other with a nasal tone. Since we understand both of them equally well, we know that the oral and nasalized vowels are merely individual variations, not separate phonemes. Such alternative pronunciations that do not affect meaning are called ALLOPHONES[2].

A complete list of Italian phonemes is found on page 120. In your study you will learn to read and write these symbols fluently. Locate the list now so that you can find it readily when it is needed.

Some customs to observe when writing in the IPA:

- Writing a word or text in the IPA is called transcribing it; the result is called an IPA transcription.
- Within the normal context of a sentence, enclose IPA symbols in slashes, / /, or square brackets [ ].
- Slashes or brackets are not needed for individual words within a transcription.
- IPA transcriptions contain only what can be heard, therefore, silent letters are omitted.
- Punctuation is not used.
- Capitalization is not used because upper case letters may be IPA symbols with special sounds.

---

1 From Greek *phōnē*, sound, voice.
2 From Greek *allos*, other.

What kind of transcription one makes depends on how much detail is desired. A PHONETIC or NARROW TRANSCRIPTION records the speech of one or more individuals with as much detail as a stranger would need to replicate it. A PHONEMIC or BROAD TRANSCRIPTION records speech in a more general way and assumes some familiarity with the language.

Phonetic, narrow transcriptions are enclosed in square brackets and show details. For instance, because every Italian D is spoken with the tongue touching the upper teeth, a narrow transcription of *da* would use the dental diacritic, thus, [da̪]. Phonemic, broad transcriptions are enclosed in slashes, and they assume a general familiarity with the language, such as the use of a dental D in Italian. A broad transcription of *da* is /da/. This book uses broad transcriptions.

Orthography

ORTHOGRAPHY[3] is the written aspect of a language: spelling, how sounds are spelled, and what spellings are accepted as correct.

In some languages the spelling of every word clearly shows what sounds are in the word. Hawaiian and Spanish are good examples, and we could say that they are "phonetically spelled," or nearly so. An example of the other extreme might be Chinese, where written symbols have no relationship to pronunciation. Most languages, like English, are between those two extremes.

It takes years for school children to learn correct spelling in English, because the relationship between pronunciation and orthography is unreliable and inconsistent. Italian school children have a much easier time. Once they learn the sound and appearance of a syllable like *"co-,"* they know that it will always look and sound the same. Italian schools do not have spelling bees because they would be pointless.

In Italian, just as in English, two letters may be used to spell a single sound. The two letters make up a DIGRAPH.[4] Example: CH spells the sound of /k/ in *orchestra*.

There is a difference between English and Italian in the treatment of doubled consonants. In English, doubling a letter does not affect the sound: for example, the sound of /t/ is exactly the same in "better" as in "beater." But in Italian a doubled consonant is prolonged, or doubly pronounced, as we would do in the phrase "slim man." Such a doubly pronounced consonant is called a GEMINATE.[5] English double consonants are never geminated within a word, but Italian double consonants are always geminated.

In discussing the sound, meaning and appearance of words, these terms and concepts are useful:

- SYNONYMS[6] are words so identical in meaning that one can substitute for another in some circumstances. Example: "speedy" and "quick."

- HOMONYMS[7] are words that look (and perhaps sound) the same but have different origins and meanings. Example: "bass" (a singer) and "bass" (a fish).

- HOMOPHONES sound the same but have different meanings. Example: "not" and "knot." Some homonyms are also homophones, but others are not.

---

[3]From Greek *ortho-*, correct, and *graph*, write.
[4]From Greek, *di-*, two, and *graphē*, write.
[5]From Latin *geminus*, twin.

[6]From Greek *sun-*, with, similar, and *onoma*, name.
[7]From Greek *homos*, same.

Vowels

VOWELS[8] are speech sounds in which the air flows out of the mouth unimpeded. As the air comes up from the vocal folds, the vocal tone resonates throughout the VOCAL TRACT, which is the name given to all of the cavities of the throat, mouth and nose. Our articulators partially control the shape of the vocal tract, for example, by lifting the tongue or by dropping the jaw. Changes in these adjustments change how the tone resonates in the vocal tract and what vowel quality the tone has. Vowels differ from each other because of the different overtones that are produced in the vocal tract.

In theory, the speech organs could adjust in an infinite number of ways and produce an infinite number of different vowels. In practical terms, every language selects a certain number of vowels that are recognized as phonemes. There is no absolute definition of any vowel; rather, vowels are defined in contrast to each other. Each vowel allows some range of variations in its formation, as long as it can be distinguished from the others.

Unless we are using scientific instruments to measure the overtones, we identify individual vowels mainly by comparing them to other vowels. Every vowel can be described by answering these questions:

- Is the vowel primarily formed by the tongue, the lips or both?

- How large, relatively, is the opening formed by the tongue or lips?

- Is this vowel, when spoken, relatively long or short?

The answers to these questions are enough to give each vowel a reasonably accurate description.

BRIGHT VOWELS, also called TONGUE VOWELS, are produced with the tongue moved forward and raised in the mouth. (English examples: EE, EH.) This action results in the presence of certain strong high overtones that produce the effect we call brightness in the tone. Phoneticians call these vowels FRONT VOWELS, but we avoid that terminology because it is easily confused with the concept of "forward placement" of the voice.

DARK VOWELS, also called ROUNDED VOWELS, are produced with rounded lips and a relatively relaxed tongue. (English examples: OO, OH.) They lack the distinctive high overtones of bright vowels. Phoneticians refer to BACK VOWELS, but that terminology must not be confused with voice placement.

CENTRAL VOWELS use the tongue and lips in relatively relaxed positions. (English example: AH.)

When one speaks of raising the tongue or rounding the lips, one must immediately ask: how much? The IPA chart on page 119 shows several terms that phoneticians use to designate the size of mouth openings required by the various vowels: close, close-mid, open-mid and open. Finer distinctions can be made with the words "tense" and "lax," but that terminology may be disagreeable to singers.

In this book about sounds, "vowel" always means a vowel sound, not a vowel letter. If a letter is meant, the specific letter will be printed in uppercase.

Human beings are able to produce many different vowel sounds, but each language uses only a few. Spanish, for instance, uses only five vowel phonemes, and Italian uses 7. Most English speakers use between 12 and 15 phonemes.

In this book you will find no diagrams to show tongue placement. Chapter 4 simply describes what the tongue touches and feels for each vowel. Vowels are best determined in comparison with each other by using the senses of touch and hearing. Efforts to form the tongue into specific shapes usually fail, leading to confusion and vocal tension.

[8]Through French, from Latin vōx, voice.

As vowels progress from close to open, one or more of the following things happen to enlarge the resonant space:

- if the lips are rounded, they open by degrees until there is no rounding;

- if the tongue was high, it lowers by degrees;

- if the jaw was not fully open, it also lowers by degrees.

Some languages require more degrees of opening and some fewer; Spanish has only three, and French and Italian have four. English has five distinct degrees of mouth opening from the smallest (EE or OO) to the most open (AH).

Say the following words aloud, focusing on the bright vowels and noticing how the resonant mouth space increases by steps from minimum to maximum:

"lease, lid, laid, led, lad ";

and then say these words with dark vowels and feel the space in your mouth increase:

"two, took, toe, taught, tar."

The following table shows these words and the IPA symbols for their main vowels (overlooking any diphthongs that sometimes occur). The middle of the table shows how the five degrees of opening are numbered in this book: levels I, II, III, IV and V, and the terms that phoneticians use for the degrees of opening.

Bright Vowels				Dark Vowels	
lease	/i/	Level I	Close	two	/u/
lid	/ɪ/	Level II	Near-close	took	/ʊ/
laid	/e/	Level III	Close-mid	toe	/o/
led	/ɛ/	Level IV	Open-mid	taught	/ɔ/
lad	/æ/	Level V	Open	tar	/ɑ/

A table of Italian vowels arranged in this way is found in Chapter 4. Level II is not used in Italian.

LONG VOWELS and SHORT VOWELS are also distinguished in Italian, but not in the same way as in English. We say that there is a "long I" in "ice" and a "short I" in "ill," meaning that the vowels have different tonal qualities. We hardly notice whether one actually lasts a longer or shorter time than the other. An Italian long vowel in a stressed syllable must actually last for a longer time than a short vowel. (This is important in singing recitative, which imitates the sound of speech.) Precise time studies show that Italians distinguish between long and short vowels even in rapid conversation; the difference is far greater in slow or emphatic speech. Chapter 4 explains vowel length and the simple spelling rules that indicate length or shortness.

Diphthongs

A DIPHTHONG[9] is a complex speech sound that begins with one vowel and moves toward another vowel within the same syllable. The listener perceives the whole diphthong as a unit. For example: "count" contains the vowels /a/ and /ʊ/, but the listener hears one diphthong rather than two vowels.

An English diphthong may be spelled with one or two letters that have little relationship to the sound of the diphthong. In Italian diphthongs, the letters always show clearly what sounds are being spoken.

In Chapter 6 we analyze Italian diphthongs as FALLING DIPHTHONGS, meaning that they move from a stronger to a weaker vowel. The first vowel, which is stressed more and held longer, is called the MAIN VOWEL. In singing, the main vowel fills up almost all of the time given to the syllable. The second vowel, which is clear but quick, is called the OFF-GLIDE. In singing, the off-glide comes at the end of a note or group of notes sung to that syllable.

In Italian the final vowel of one word and the initial vowel of another often combine into one syllable called a SYNALEPHA,[10] as will be described in Chapter 7. (This also happens often in Spanish but never in English, French or German.) In a synalepha there may be one or two subordinate vowels before and after the main vowel.

Semivowels

A SEMIVOWEL is formed when the speech organs move from one vowel position to another so quickly that the first vowel is heard as a kind of consonant. Examples in English are the Y in "you" /ju/ and the W in "we" /wi/. Italian has the same two semivowels as English, spelled with the letters I and U.

Some Italian scholars call these sounds "rising diphthongs," meaning that they move from a weaker to a stronger vowel. This book adopts the standpoint of the Italian phonetician Canepàri (1999): Syllables like /ja/ and /wa/ resemble syllables like /la/ that consist of consonant + vowel, and they are therefore not diphthongs (*Manuale*, p. 144). We agree that such syllables are combinations of semivowel + vowel.

The IPA now describes /j/ and /w/ as approximants, a term that is explained in the next section. This author believes that the older term "semivowel" is more sympathetic to singers.

Consonants

CONSONANTS are speech sounds which involve a closed, or somewhat restricted vocal tract. There is an interference or obstruction to the breath stream, either stopping it momentarily, diverting it from its usual path through the center of the mouth, or producing a sound of turbulent air (friction).

> In this book about sounds, "consonant" always means a consonant *sound,* not a consonant letter. If a letter is meant, the specific letter is printed in upper-case.

Every consonant can be described by answering three questions:

• Is it spoken with the vocal folds (vocal cords) vibrating or not?

• In what way does the consonant articulation interfere with breath flow?

• Where in the vocal tract does the interference take place?

Each question involves a particular set of terms, which are explained below.

VOICED CONSONANTS are made with vibrating vocal folds. They have pitches and are as much a part of our singing as vowels are. VOICELESS CONSONANTS are merely noises made by the mouth or throat. Because the vocal folds are not vibrating, voiceless consonants have no distinct pitches.

---

[9]From Greek *di-*, two, *phthongos*, sound.
[10]Greek: *syn-*, with, *alepha*, smear.

Consonants play a role in vocal music similar to that of percussion instruments in orchestral music. Voiced consonants are like the instruments with definite pitches, such as chimes and marimbas. Voiceless consonants resemble the instruments without definite pitches, such as cymbals and drums.

The second main question asks how the breath stream issues from the body. The relevant categories for Italian are: plosive, nasal, trill, tap, fricative and approximant. (These terms are found in the left-hand column of the IPA chart of consonants.) Within these categories, the sounds that can be prolonged are called CONTINUANTS.

PLOSIVES stop the breath stream completely, so that for a brief instant no air at all passes through either the mouth or the nose, and then release it. Examples: /b/ /k/. If an audible burst of air comes after a voiceless stop, it is said to be ASPIRATED.[11] Good English diction requires aspiration, but it is not typical of Italian.

NASALS are heard when the air stream is diverted completely through the nose instead of the mouth. Italian has four nasals, /m/, /n/, /ŋ/ and /ɲ/, as described in Chapter 5; all other Italian consonants are ORAL CONSONANTS.

A TRILL interrupts the breath stream repeatedly. A TAP interrupts the breath stream only once and does so more lightly than a plosive. Italian has one of each, and both are represented by the letter R. (Phoneticians have a name for the many variations of R: RHOTIC, after the Greek letter *rho*. Other rhotic sounds include the English/American R, the French uvular R, etc.)

FRICATIVES nearly close off the air stream but let enough air pass through to produce a sound of air turbulence. Examples: /v/ /f/. The IPA chart shows that fricatives are the largest family of consonants, but English and Italian use fewer than half of them. Fricatives that have a hissing sound are also called SIBILANTS. Examples: /s/ /z/.

If the breath stream is not stopped or made turbulent, but is still somewhat restricted, the resulting sound is called an APPROXIMANT. (The term comes from two articulators that "approximate" but touch lightly or not at all.) Italian has two of these that are called LATERAL APPROXIMANTS because they divert the air around the sides of the raised tongue. Examples: /l/, /ʎ/. As stated above, the IPA also describes /j/ and /w/ as approximants; we prefer to call them semivowels.

AFFRICATES are compound sounds that consist of a plosive and a sibilant pronounced as one unit. Example: English CH /tʃ/. The IPA chart does not show affricates as a separate class because of the many possible combinations.

The third main question asks for the PLACE OF ARTICULATION for each consonant, the point where the breath is diverted or obstructed from its free flow. Books about speech usually explain this with diagrams, but it is more useful to explore our own articulators by the sense of touch.

With your mouth closed, lower the TIP (or apex) of your tongue so that it touches the inside surface of the lower teeth. Just behind the tip, the surface of the tongue is called the BLADE (or lamina). With the teeth closed and the tip still down, the blade is touching a convex ridge that contains the sockets of the upper teeth; it is called the ALVEOLAR RIDGE (the stressed syllable is *-ve-*). Farther back, the upper surface of the tongue is called the BODY (or dorsum). Behind the alveolar ridge the body contacts a narrow area that is referred to as POSTALVEOLAR (or prepalatal), but it does not have clear boundaries. The roof of the mouth has three named areas, in order from front to back: PALATAL (where the tongue feels the bony hard palate); VELAR (where the tongue feels soft tissue); and UVULAR (seen with a mirror, hanging down at the back of the mouth).

To test which consonants are voiced:
- touch your throat and feel the vibration of your larynx; or
- stop one ear with your finger and hear the buzzing sound in your throat.

Try this with the sound /v/, then with /f/.

/v/ produces buzzing vibrations, but voiceless /f/ does not.

---

[11]From Latin *ad-*, on, and *spirare*, to breathe.

This term. . .	Means that the place of articulation is between. . .
BILABIAL	Both lips
LABIODENTAL	Lower lip and the upper incisors
DENTAL	Tongue tip and the inside surface of the upper incisors
ALVEOLAR	Tongue tip or blade and the alveolar ridge
POSTALVEOLAR	Tongue blade or body and the area behind the alveolar ridge
PALATAL	Tongue body and the hard palate
VELAR	Tongue body (back) and the soft palate

When you have located all of the articulators described above, there will be no mysteries in their technical names. Familiarity with these terms helps us to be aware of the movements that the articulators perform in speaking and singing.

In Chapter 5 each consonant is described with three terms that correspond to the three main questions. For example, /d/ is a "voiced dental plosive," and no other consonant matches that description.

Syllables

SYLLABLES are segments that, singly or joined together, make up words. In sung English or Italian every syllable has a NUCLEUS of a vowel or diphthong, which may be preceded and/or followed by one or more consonants. In spoken English a consonant can form the nucleus of a syllable, as in the second syllable of "kitten," but this does not occur in Italian. To state the obvious, a sung word must have at least as many notes as it has syllables; a four syllable word cannot be sung on a phrase of only three notes.

Along with the vowel or diphthong nucleus, a syllable may contain one or more consonants. The most typical Italian syllable consists of one consonant and one vowel. Such a syllable, ending with a vowel, is called an OPEN SYLLABLE. A more typical English syllable is a CLOSED SYLLABLE, one that ends with a consonant. Relatively few Italian syllables end with consonants.

Both Italian and English make clear distinctions between stronger (louder) and weaker (softer) syllables. We will call them STRESSED and UNSTRESSED SYLLABLES. We do not speak of "accented" syllables because we want to use the word ACCENT for the diacritics used in some languages, as in the Italian *sarà*.

In music it is usually easy to recognize a stressed syllable because it falls on a strong beat of the measure. The standard IPA method of indicating stress is to place a stress symbol / ' / before the strongest (stressed) syllable. If needed, a secondary stress symbol / , / is placed before the next strongest syllable. This book uses a method that was introduced by Berton Coffin (1982): the vowel of the stressed syllable is underlined. A stronger stress can be shown with a double underline and a weaker stress with a single underline. By directing attention to vowels, this method corresponds to the way singers think.

Chapter 3 provides rules for dividing words into syllables because some pronunciation rules depend on knowing whether a particular sound occurs at the beginning or end of a syllable. A vowel or consonant can be:

- INITIAL, at the beginning of a word or syllable;

- MEDIAL, in the middle; or

- FINAL, at the end.

Some rules affect consonants that are INTERVOCALIC, between two vowels.

Chapter 2: The Italian Language

Learning the Italian language opens the door to a colorful world of art and music. Millions of tourists visit Italy every year to admire Italian art treasures, to savor the food and wine, to view the landscapes and historic sites, and to enjoy concerts and operas.

Track 1

In the European tradition of classical music, all musicians agree to use Italian words for the most basic terms, such as *allegro* and *forte*. As singers, we recognize that our basic concepts of artistic singing come from Italy. An Italian expression, *bel canto,* beautiful singing, sums up the vocal ideals that we strive for.

Romance Languages and Modern Italian

As a speaker of English, you will recognize many Italian words. The grammar of English is different from that of Italian in many ways, but many words that we use daily have their origin in Latin, which is also the basis of the modern Italian language.

Two millennia ago the most powerful political force in Europe was the Roman Empire. Latin was its official language and Christianity became its official religion in 330. Even after the Roman Empire collapsed politically, the Latin language remained important in western Europe, which was dominated by the Roman Catholic Church.

As centuries passed, written Latin and church Latin changed relatively little simply because writing lends permanence that spoken words do not have. For many centuries Latin remained the language of international scholarship and diplomacy. By 1100 there was a university at Bologna, considered the first in Europe. As universities were founded in other countries—Paris (by 1170), Cambridge (1208), Salamanca, Spain (1243)—they were originally Latin speaking communities of young men who had learned Latin in the "grammar schools" maintained by churches.

Meanwhile, the language of daily life was not limited to Latin. The "vulgar" languages spoken in various parts of the former Empire were evolving into what we now call ROMANCE LANGUAGES. The principal Romance languages, listed from west to east, are: Portuguese, Spanish, French, Italian and Romanian. Other Romance languages, such as Ladino and Catalan, are spoken by smaller numbers of people.

Each of the Romance languages contains influences from the indigenous peoples who were conquered by the Romans, from Latin, and from other invaders who either passed through the countries or settled down and stayed. French and Italian were influenced by Germanic invaders from the north and east.

The earliest written evidence of the Italian language is found in a legal document concerning a land dispute in 960. The document is written in Latin, but the witnesses' sworn statement is quoted in Italian, clear evidence of the way that ordinary people in central Italy were speaking.

Among the first preserved literary works in Italian are brief devotional texts by Francesco d'Assisi (Saint Francis of Assisi, 1182–1226), among them his *"Cantico delle creature"* (Canticle of the Creatures). The generation following St. Francis felt his influence and produced the first flowering of Italian lyric poetry.

The first major literary work in Italian is regarded as a milestone of world literature: *Divina commedia,* by Dante Alighieri (1265–1321). In contrast to tragedy, Dante's "comedy" has a sad beginning and a happy ending. It tells the story of a confused and grieving man who is taken on a visionary tour of Hell, Purgatory and Heaven. Its imaginative depiction of those places still influences the popular notions that show up today in jokes and cartoons about Hell and Heaven.

Dante wrote his immense work, 14,233 lines of rhymed verse, in the dialect of Florence, capital of the region of Tuscany. This fact alone gave the Tuscan dialect, *toscano*, great prestige as the most beautiful and elegant form of Italian. It became the standard for written Italian for several centuries, significantly slowing the evolution of the language. Today, Italians still read *Divina commedia* in school, with explanatory notes but in the original. In contrast, Chaucer's *Canterbury Tales*, written in the Middle English of the late 1300s, must be translated into modern English for us to read. Literary English has changed much more in six centuries than has literary Italian.

After the defeat of Rome in 476 most of the peninsula of Italy stayed under alien rule for almost 14 centuries. Boundaries shifted and foreign powers came and went. Modern independent Italy came into being in 1861 under King Vittorio Emmanuele II of Savoy. In 1870 Italian troops captured Rome from the rule of the Pope, and Rome became the capital of a united Italian peninsula.

Dialects and Standard Italian

In a country where most people stay near their parents' homes all their lives, they develop particular local ways of speaking called DIALECTS. In Italy many cities, even small ones, have distinctive dialects that are difficult for outsiders to imitate or to understand. The varieties of Italian that are spoken in Sicily and Naples in the south and Venice and Milan in the north are so distinct that their enthusiasts call them separate languages, not dialects. For example, a current Milanese-Italian dictionary runs to more than 900 pages.

Some famous Italian songs have been written in regional languages. Rossini's *La regata veneziana* (Venetian Boat Race), for instance, is a song cycle written in *veneto*, which is spoken in Venice. The most famous of all Italian popular songs, di Capua's " 'O sole mio" (My Sun), is in *napoletano*, spoken in Naples (see page 114).

The national unity that came in 1870 brought with it the problem of establishing a common language that all Italians would understand. That was solved after 1950 when the popularity of television caused a standard Italian to be carried into every home. Italy has no linguistic academy and the government does not legislate about language matters, but the national broadcasting system, RAI, developed a blend of Tuscan and Roman dialects that became acceptable to everyone.

Once there was a fear that the influence of broadcasting would kill the local dialects, but that did not happen nor will it happen. Local pride has led people to cultivate their dialects with enjoyment of their distinctive qualities. As a result, many Italians have two distinct ways of speaking, using both standard Italian and a local dialect.

Italians, generally speaking, welcome whatever efforts foreigners make to speak their language. But one should be warned: the tolerant Italians may have little inclination to correct others' mistakes. You may receive a friendly, encouraging compliment about how well you speak Italian and realize later that you were making dozens of errors.

Using Italian Dictionaries

A good Italian-English dictionary is an important part of a singer's library, but: Buyer beware! Many of the smaller ones give no information at all about pronunciation. Even worse, some dictionaries and phrase books try to show Italian pronunciation with English spelling, as if all Italian sounds exist in English (but they don't!). Still others show pronunciations, but with their own, non-standardized sets of symbols.

When you buy an Italian-English dictionary, it is worthwhile to search for one that uses IPA. Availability changes from year to year, so no other recommendation can be made here.

The first pronouncing dictionary of Italian using IPA and including proper names appeared in 1999: *Dizionario di pronuncia italiana* by Luciano Canepàri (Zanichelli). It is in Italian only, and meanings are given only for homonyms. Regional variations are included, and the author indicates which pronunciations are and are not recommended as standard. Although there are some differences in style, the transcriptions will be clear to anyone who has studied this book. (Any further references to Canepàri in this book are to his *Dizionario*.)

Chapter 3: Characteristic Patterns and Sounds in Italian

Every language has typical sound patterns by which we can recognize it even without understanding a word. If we pay attention to these patterns in Italian, they will take us a long way toward sounding authentic; if we ignore them, we can speak every syllable correctly and still fail to sound Italian.

What Makes Italian Sound Italian?

Here are some ways that Italian compares with other major languages that you are likely to study as a classically trained singer:

- Italians tend to speak with much more energy than English speakers. Every first time visitor to Italy notices this national stereotype: Italians seem to talk loudly, enthusiastically and with gesticulation. Some speak softly and gently, but it is unusual to find one who mumbles. In order to sound Italian, we must be willing to speak expressively and with resonant vowel sounds. Italy is the birthplace of opera, and opera is an art of passion and overstatement!

- Italian and French strongly prefer open syllables, which end in vowels. English and German favor closed syllables, which end with consonants.

- Italian and Spanish have simple vowel patterns, with only a few different vowels to learn. English, French and German have more than twice as many vowel phonemes.

- Italian vowels, both stressed and unstressed, always keep their clear, individual qualities. Such distinctness is also typical of French, German and Spanish. This contrasts with the English language, in which unstressed vowels often fade toward neutral sounds.

- Italian single consonants are pronounced gently, as in Spanish and French, and with much less energy and expulsion of breath than are used in English and German.

- Italians do not use aspirated consonants. American choral conductors sometimes say, "Spit out your consonants," but that would strike an Italian as disgusting.

- Italian double consonants, which occur between vowels, are emphasized more than are double consonants in any of the other languages mentioned.

- In Italian, the only consonants that normally occur at the end of a word are L, M, N and (rolled) R, all of which can be sustained and sung on pitch. In English or German, almost any consonant can end a word, even a voiceless consonant.

 Track 2

- Italians connect their words in a *legato* manner. Except for the brief silences caused by some voiceless double consonants, the sound of Italian is continuous and words flow into each other, as they do in French. English and German speakers prefer clear articulations between words, even gaps, rather than connections.

Serious voice study often begins with easy arias in Italian. While this is generally a fine thing, it often leads to two false ideas: that you can sing well without clearly understanding the words, and that Italian is easy to sing.

The first idea is seen to be false when you realize that the purpose of singing is to communicate an emotional message to an audience. To do that, you must understand the words you are singing perfectly. To help you toward that goal, every example word in this book is translated. When you practice pronouncing a word, you can also see its translation in the same glance.

The other idea is also false: Italian is a language of precise sounds. Because Italian has a simple vowel system, every vowel is clear and every mistake is noticeable.

The Alphabet — *L'Alfabeto* /alfabeːto/

The Italian alphabet contains only 21 letters. The following table shows the letters, their names and the pronunciation of the names. To the right are words that are used to help clarify the spelling of a word, for instance, when talking on the telephone. Most are city names; notice that certain famous cities have English names that are different from their Italian names.

	Name	Pronunciation	Al telefono /tele̯fono/	
A	a	/a/[1]	Ancona	/ãŋkoːna/
B	bi	/bi/	Bari	/baːɾi/
C	ci	/tʃi/	Como	/kɔːmo/
D	di	/di/	Domodossola	/domodɔsːsola/
E	e	/ɛ/	Empoli	/empoli/
F	effe	/ɛfːfe/	Firenze (Florence)	/fiɾɛntse/
G	gi	/dʒi/	Genova (Genoa)	/dʒɛːnova/
H	acca	/akːka/	hotel	/otɛl/
I	i	/i/	Imola	/iːmola/
L	elle	/ɛlːle/	Livorno	/livorno/
M	emme	/ɛmːme/	Milano (Milan)	/milaːno/
N	enne	/ɛnːne/	Napoli (Naples)	/naːpoli/
O	o	/ɔ/	Otranto	/ɔːtranto/
P	pi	/pi/	Palermo	/palɛrmo/
Q	cu	/ku/	quarto (fourth)	/kwarto/
R	erre	/ɛrːre/	Roma (Rome)	/roːma/
S	esse	/ɛsːse/	Savona	/savoːna/
T	ti	/ti/	Torino (Turin)	/toriːno/
U	u	/u/	Udine	/uːdine/
V	vu	/vu/	Venezia (Venice)	/venɛtːtsja/
Z	zeta	/dzɛːta/	Zeta	/dzɛːta/

The other five letters occur in foreign words but they do not belong to the Italian alphabet.

	Name	Pronunciation	Al telefono /tele̯fono/
J	i lunga	/illuŋga/	i lunga
K	cappa	/kapːpa/	cappa
W	doppia vu	/dopːpjavu/	Washington
Y	ipsilon	/ipsilon/	York
X	ics	/iks/	ics

[1]Beginning here, example words are given with their IPA transcriptions. If you encounter unfamiliar symbols, either imitate your teacher's pronunciation or postpone speaking the words aloud until you have learned the material in the next chapters. It is better to skip words than to form bad habits by practicing incorrect pronunciations.

Track 3

Accents — *Gl'Accenti*

Two forms of accent are used: GRAVE ACCENT (`) and ACUTE ACCENT ( ). Their Italian names, respectively, are *l'accento grave* /atːtʃɛnto graːve/ and *accento acuto* /akuːto/.

In former times, publishers used only the grave accent for all vowels, and some still follow that policy. More careful publishers use an acute accent to make a distinction (discussed in Chapter 4) between *e chiuso*, closed E, printed as é, and *e aperto*, open E, printed as è. Still others use an acute accent over three final vowels that are relatively closed; é, í, ú. (Stressed final ó never occurs.)

Written accents are used consistently for two purposes:

1) to indicate that the final vowel of a word is stressed:

già	/dʒa/	already
tornerà	/tornera/	she/he will return
il[2] caffè	/kafːfɛ/	coffee
perché (or: perchè)	/perke/	because
finí (or: finì)	/finiː/	he/she/it finished
amerò	/amerɔ/	I-will-love
piú (or: più)	/pju/	more

2) to distinguish between monosyllabic homonyms. In most such cases the two words are pronounced identically.

che	/ke/	which	chè	/ke/	because
da	/da/	from	dà	/da/	gives
di	/di/	of	dí	/di/	day
e	/e/	and	è	/ɛ/	is (Notice!)
la	/la/	the	là	/la/	there
ne	/ne/	of it; of them	né	/ne/	neither, nor
si	/si/	oneself	sí	/si/	yes

Written Italian sometimes uses an accent to differentiate between homonyms that are stressed differently. This is helpful to someone who is reading aloud, but unfortunately, it is not usually done.

ancora	/aŋkoːra/	yet
l'ancora, l'àncora	/aŋkora/	anchor
i principi	/printʃiːpi/	principles
i principi, príncipi	/printʃipi/	princes

Older editions sometimes used an accent mark when /i/ is stressed before a final vowel. Again, this is optional.

| la follia, la follía | /folliːa/ | madness |

---

[2]If an example word is a noun, the definite article (the) will be given because it reveals the gender of the noun and assists in adding the word to your Italian vocabulary. Usually, only one meaning is given; a dictionary may give several.

A CIRCUMFLEX ACCENT, *accento circonflesso* /tʃirkonflɛsso/, was sometimes used in older editions to show that a letter was omitted.

| dormia, dormîa, dormiva | /dormiːa dormiːva/ | he/she slept |
| udii, udî | /udiː udiː/ | I heard |

Syllabication — *La Sillabazione* /silːlabatːtsjoːne/

Track 4

A singer often needs to know how to divide a word into syllables. The printed words in musical scores are not always hyphenated, and hyphenation may be inconsistent or incorrect. Sight reading and practicing are hampered if the singer is unsure which sounds belong to which notes.

Separation of syllables in Italian follows certain procedures that are different from those used in English. Every syllable contains one vowel or diphthong. The syllable may begin with the vowel, or it may begin with one, two or three consonants and/or semivowels ahead of the vowel. The syllable usually ends with the vowel or diphthong. A syllable may end with a consonant in these cases:

- if the consonant is L, M, N or R;

- if it is the first consonant of a pair of doubled consonants;

- or in a few other cases mentioned below.

The following words show various ways that syllables are formed. Notice the first syllable of each word.

Vowel alone:

| eco, e-co | /ɛːko/[3] | echo |

Vowel + the first of a pair of consonants:

| ecco, ec-co | /ɛkːko/ | here it is |

Diphthong alone:

| aura, au-ra | /au.ra/ | light breeze |

Consonant + vowel:

| luna, lu-na | /luːna/ | moon |

Consonant + diphthong

| rauco, rau-co | /rau.ko/ | hoarse |

Two consonants + vowel

| spumone, spu-mo-ne | /spu.moːne/ | name of a dessert |

Two consonants + vowel + M:

| stampa, stam-pa | /stam.pa/ | printing |

Two consonants + semivowel + vowel + L:

| squallore, squal-lo-re | /skwalːloːre/ | misery |

---

[3] In IPA transcriptions a lengthening symbol /ː/ always marks the boundary between syllables. A period can be used to show syllabication, as it is on the following pages, but it is not usually needed.

Every example word given above ends in a vowel. A few short words end in L, N or R, such as:

il	/il/	the
un	/un/	a

Also, some words adopted from other languages end in other consonants, including the four directional words *nord* /nɔrd/ (N) , *sud* /sud/ (S), *est* /ɛst/ (E), *ovest* /ɔːvɛst/ (W).

Syllabication in Italian always follows the principles just given. The principles can be re-stated in the form of rules, as follows.

- <u>One</u> consonant between vowels belongs to the following syllable.

amato, a-ma-to	/a.maːto/	beloved
solitudine, so-li-tu-di-ne	/so.li.tuːdi.ne/	solitude

- <u>Double</u> consonant letters are divided between the syllables:

inno, in-no	/inːno/	hymn
avvezzo, av-vez-zo	/avːvetːtso/	accustomed

- <u>Two</u> dissimilar consonant letters belong to the following syllable:

vaghe, va-ghe	/vaːge/	lovely
potrà, po-trà	/po.tra/	will-be-able

But they are separated if the first of the two is L, M, N or R:

alfine, al-fi-ne	/al.fiːne/	finally
impero, im-pe-ro	/im.pɛːro/	empire
conforto, con-for-to	/kon.fɔr.to/	comfort

And two dissimilar consonants are divided in other rare cases where it is felt that two consecutive consonants cannot be pronounced together.

abnorme, ab-nor-me	/ab.nɔr.me/	extraordinary
il tecnico, tec-ni-co	/tɛk.ni.ko/	expert

- <u>Three</u> consonant letters: if the first is L, M, N or R, it belongs to the preceding syllable, the others to the following one.

altro, al-tro	/al.tro/	other
sempre, sem-pre	/sɛm.pre/	always

In all other cases the first of three consonant letters is an S, and the three consonants belong to the following syllable.

vostro, vo-stro	/vɔ.stro/	your (plural)
disgrazia, di-sgra-zia	/di.zgratːtsja/	misfortune

Finally, in some situations a diphthong can be split into two syllables, either because the composer wrote it that way in the music or because a run of quick notes will sound better if the second vowel of the diphthong is sung on the last one or two notes of the run. This will be discussed in Chapter 6.

Chapter 7 will also discuss how two or more syllables combine into one if there are no consonants to separate them.

How Words Change Their Forms

Italian words often change their forms to improve the rhythm of a phrase or because a poet wants to have a certain number of syllables in a poetic line. Also, some word forms change with the centuries, sometimes becoming simpler, but not always. Word forms change in several different ways.

CONTRACTION is the shortening of a word by omitting letters (sounds) in the middle. Some common examples that appear in opera librettos are:

 Track 5

cuore, core	/kwɔːɾe kɔːɾe/	heart
egli, ei	/eʎːʎi ei/	he
belli, bei	/bɛlːli bɛi/	beautiful (m. pl.)
quali, quai	/kwaːli kwai/	what

ELISION is the omission of a final vowel indicated by an apostrophe. Elision is obligatory in some cases and optional in others.

un'opera (una)	/unɔːpeɾa/	an opera
onest'uomo (onesto)	/onɛstwɔːmo/	honest man
dovrebb'essere (dovrebbe)	/dovrɛbːbɛsːseɾe/	ought to be

COMPOUND WORDS are of two kinds.

(1) An elision can become so common that the two words come to be accepted as a compound word that is written without an apostrophe.

gentiluomo (gentile)	/dʒentilwɔːmo/	gentleman

(2) A pronoun may be attached to the end of certain verb forms, whether the combination is obligatory or optional.

affittasi (si affitta)	/afːfitːtasi/	"for rent"
parlargliene (parlare a lui/lei di questo)	/parlarʎene/	to talk to him about it

Italian can present some puzzling combinations. Here is a compound word that is elided to the next word:

gliel'indicai (lo indicai a lui)	/ʎelindikai/	I pointed it out to him

TRUNCATION is the omission of a word ending, which may be a final vowel, final syllable or even two syllables. No apostrophe is used, but the remainder must end in L, M, N or R. (Notice that a word like *bocca* cannot be truncated because the remainder would end in /k/.) The shortened word may precede another word or be final in the sentence. Truncations are common in poetry. Composers often use their discretion to truncate a word or not so that it will suit the melody they want to write.

dove son? (sono)	/doːve son/	where are they?
una gran festa (grande)	/una gran fɛsta/	a grand festival
v'entrar (vi entrarono)	/ventrar/	they entered here

(This could also be read as *vi entrare*, to enter here.)

Linking, which is described in detail in Chapter 7 as the normal legato style of Italian speech, shows up in one orthographic form: the addition of D to a one-letter word before a vowel. A final D appears to break the rule that a syllable can only end in L, M, N or R, but the D actually links phonetically with the following vowel to form a new syllable.

ad altri	/a.da̲l.tri/	to others
gioia ed amor	/dʒɔ̲ːja e.da.mo̲ːr/	joy and love

Stress / *L'Accento.* /latːtʃe̲nto/

Italian sounds lively and emotional to most outsiders, and syllabic stress plays an important role in creating this impression. Singing without attention to correct and clear stresses leads to a general blandness that falls far short of our ultimate goal, which is expressive communication.

> Expressive emphasis in English is mainly a matter of consonants, but emphasis is achieved in Italian mainly through vowels. It is an interesting experiment to speak English with strong, emphatic vowels but gentle, soft consonants. Attempting to do this can help us understand why Italians sound as they do (and why Italian is a wonderful language for singing!).

Every word of two or more syllables has one syllable with the main stress of the word. Main stresses are usually easy to find in music because strong syllables are on strong rhythmic beats. For situations where the stress is unclear, one needs to know the common patterns described here.

To locate stress in an Italian word, one counts the syllables from the end. About 4% of Italian words are stressed on the final syllable, about 50% on the next-to-last syllable, about 10% on the third-from-last syllable. The remainder are mostly one syllable words, including common words that occur very often.

Track 6

Final syllable stress results in a "truncated (shortened) word," *parola tronca* /paɾɔ̲ːla tro̲˜ka/. If the truncated word ends with a stressed vowel, it is marked with a written accent. Some truncated words have old forms that end in -*de*; notice that the truncated form has an accent mark, but the longer form does not.

Signor, Signore	/siɲːɲo̲ːr siɲːɲo̲ːre/	sir
perché	/perke̲/	why, because
ferí	/feɾi̲/	wounded
pietà, pietade	/pjeta̲ pjeta̲ːde/	pity

Penultimate (next to last) syllable stress is normal in Italian, and it results in a "plain word," *parola piana* /paɾɔ̲ːla pja̲ːna/. Here are examples of plain words with from two to six syllables:

pizza	/pi̲ːtsa/	pizza
spaghetti	/spage̲ːti/	spaghetti
insalata	/insala̲ːta/	salad
locomotiva	/lokomoti̲ːva/	locomotive engine
immagineremmo	/imːmadʒineɾe̲mːmo/	we would imagine

Some words and some verb forms end with a stressed diphthong. In some cases a composer will decide to divide the diphthong into two syllables.

| co-lei, co-le-i | /koˈlɛi kolˈɛːi/ | she, her |
| vor-rei, vor-re-i | /vorːˈrɛi vorːˈrɛːi/ | I would like |

Antepenultimate (third from last) syllable stress results in a "slid word," *parola sdrucciola* /zdrutːtʃola/. Publishers seldom mark such stresses. Track 7

camera	/ˈkaːmeɾa/	room
medico	/ˈmɛːdiko/	physician
opera	/ˈɔːpeɾa/	opera
baritono	/baˈɾiːtono/	baritone

There are no reliable rules for recognizing words whose basic form has antepenultimate stress. However, there are certain grammatical endings that result in *parole sdrucciole*, for instance:

- Adjectives ending in *-abile, -esimo, -evole, -ibile, -issimo.*

cantabile	/kanˈtaːbile/	singable
piacevole	/pjatˈʃeːvole/	pleasant
fortissimo	/forˈtisːsimo/	very strong

- Some verb infinitives that end in *-ere*, but not all.

| credere | /ˈkrɛːdeɾe/ | to believe |
| offendere | /ofˈfɛndeɾe/ | to offend |

- Third person plural (they) verbs.

cantano	/ˈkantano/	they sing
vedono	/ˈveːdono/	they see
offenderebbero	/ofˈfɛndeɾɛbːbeɾo/	they would offend

Fourth-last syllable stress is even rarer and results in "twice-slid words," *parole bisdrucciole* /bizdrutːtʃole/. These include the third person plural forms of certain verbs with infinitives in *-are* and also verbs to which pronoun objects have been attached.

| esaminano | /eˈzaːminano/ | they examine |
| dateglielo (lo date a lui/lei) | /ˈdaːteʎːʎelo/ | give it to him/her |

In the case of a proper name, one may have to learn the proper stress from someone who knows the name or else look it up in a pronouncing dictionary.

Figaro	/ˈfiːgaɾo/	operatic role
Bartolo	/ˈbartolo/	operatic role
Bartoli	/ˈbartoli/	singer
Cenerentola	/tʃeneˈrɛntola/	Cinderella (opera)

Stresses Against the Music

Composers go against normal stress knowingly sometimes, trusting us to work with the ambiguous rhythms that result.

Le nozze di Figaro (The Marriage of Figaro) and other operas by Da Ponte and Mozart have many phrases like the following, which is sung by Figaro in the recitative before his first aria:

"...e a veder schietto..."   /eavvﻉder skjﻉːto/   and to see clearly

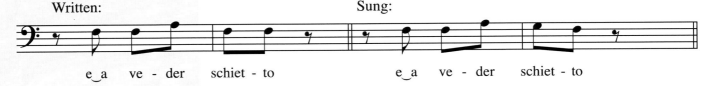

Veder is truncated from the verb *vedere*, which is normally stressed on the second syllable. In the truncated form, the second syllable keeps its stress, even though this means that two stressed syllables, *-der schiet-* are side by side. The music moves quickly, but even so, the performer must give *-der* a slight stress and avoid stressing the previous syllable, *ve-*. In this case, Mozart found a way to stress both syllables, first, by giving the *-der* a leap upward and then by putting the *schiet-* on a note that will be sung as an appoggiatura on the pitch G, not F.

In the chorus *"Va, pensiero"* (see page 111) Verdi used the word *"simile,"* normally stressed on the first syllable, and gave it a strong musical stress on the second syllable. Such cases are rare in Italian, and one must accept them as a privilege of genius.

Vowel and Consonant Length

In English a long vowel usually has a different quality (tone color) from a short vowel. The difference is phonemic, as for instance, "mate" with long A is different from "mat" with short A. As it is usually spoken, the first vowel is probably not really longer than the other, measured in milliseconds.

Vowel quality and length are independent of each other in Italian. Any vowel can be either long or short, and a long vowel actually lasts a fraction of a second longer than the short vowels around it. The difference between long and short vowels is not phonemic, but your Italian will not sound authentic without it. In IPA, the symbol /ː/ placed after the vowel shows that it is long.

Consonants can also be long in Italian (not in English). Double consonants sound the same as single ones in English, but they actually last longer in Italian. This can be shown in IPA by placing the lengthener /ː/ between two consonants; for instance, /tːt/ /mːm/. (Chapter 5 discusses this in detail.)

Rhythm and Syllable Length

When first learning to play an instrument, we learn to play the note values evenly; for instance, all of the eighth notes in a measure of music must be equal in length, although some are accented more than others. A more sophisticated musician knows that eighth notes in a measure may vary subtly, in length as well as in stress, according to expressive nuances.

Singers, whatever language they are singing, have to deal with rhythmic variations that are even subtler. If the consonants at the beginning of a syllable have to be anticipated, time is stolen from the preceding note or rest. If the syllable ends with a consonant, it takes up part of the note value. If the syllable contains more than one vowel, the note value must be divided between them. These are only some of the ways we continually compromise between precise musical rhythms and the much more erratic rhythms of a spoken language.

We have mentioned vowel and consonant length, and those concepts combine in SYLLABLE LENGTH. Obviously, native Italians do not have to think about syllable length, and Italian reference books often ignore it. But our Italian singing will not sound native unless we pay attention to the extra length that goes along with stress.

In Italian, all unstressed syllables are roughly equal in length, but stressed syllables are longer. One-syllable words vary, being long if they are emphatic and are followed by consonants pronounced single, but short if they are unimportant or are followed by consonants pronounced as double. (This will be explained in Chapter 7).

What does this mean to a singer? A long vowel completely fills up the value of its note. A short vowel does not, because part of the note value is given to the following consonant. (This is discussed more in Chapter 5). The distinction is greatest in singing *recitativo*, the style where singing is most like speech, but it is present in all styles.

A stressed syllable carries the emotional energy of a statement. If the syllable is open, the vowel is its expressive part, and it may be stretched and inflected with feeling:

| Non m'ami? | /non maːmi/ | Don't you love me? |
| Baciami! | /baːtʃami/ | Kiss me! |

If a stressed syllable ends with a diphthong, the main vowel is expressive (the lengthener /ː/ is not used because stressed diphthongs are naturally long):

| Tu puoi! | /tu pwɔi/ | You can! |

If the stressed syllable ends in a consonant, the consonant focuses the expressive energy of the word. The consonant is lengthened rather than the vowel:

| Infatti, sí! | /infatːti si/ | Yes, in fact! |
| Per sempre! | /per sɛmpre/ | Forever! |

The examples just given are sufficient to introduce the concept of syllable length, which will become clearer with more experience.

To summarize, in a <u>stressed</u> syllable:

- A vowel is long (fills up its note value) when it is followed by a single consonant and another vowel.

- A final vowel is long (fills up its note value) at the end of a phrase or before most words, but short if the initial consonant of the next word is pronounced double (explained in Chapter 7).

- A vowel is short (and the consonant takes part of its note value) before a double consonant, before a consonant cluster beginning with S, or before these consonants, which are pronounced double, as explained in Chapter 5: GLI, GN, SC (before E or I), or Z.

The example words already used in this chapter show many examples of long and short vowels and consonants in stressed syllables.

Rhymes in Italian Poetry

Rhyme is a key factor in most traditional English poetry, so much so that poems are sometimes called "rhymes." Some standardized patterns of rhymes, such as the sonnet or rondeau, are regarded as challenges to a poet's technical skill.

Rhyme is relatively easy in Italian because so many words have identical endings. Because rhyming is so easy to do, most Italian poets take little interest in it and use mostly simple rhyme schemes. Some lines may be left unrhymed.

The poetry of operas is naturally divided into recitatives and arias. The texts of recitatives are usually unrhymed, except that there may be a pair of rhymed lines to call attention to the end of a major speech or scene, a technique that Shakespeare also used in his plays. Aria texts are usually rhymed. In the *da capo* arias of the Baroque period, the two parts of the aria were often linked together by rhyming the last line of the first stanza with the last line of the second.

Rhythms in Italian Poetry

The rhythms of English poetry are organized in terms of meter, that is, the arrangement of stressed and unstressed syllables in a line. For instance, a typical line from a play by Shakespeare contains five "feet," and each foot consists of a weak and a strong syllable. (Of course, Shakespeare varied that basic pattern with great flexibility.)

Italian poetry developed differently because of the strong influence of Latin verse, which is organized in patterns of long and short syllables rather than stresses. As a result, Italian verse is organized by the number of syllables in the line.

Each line length has a name based on the syllable count. The favorite line lengths are the seven-syllable *settenàrio* and the eleven-syllable *endecasíllabo*.

The placement of syllables within a line may vary, but the penultimate syllable must be stressed. A *settenàrio* has a stress on the sixth syllable, and a line with a stress on the sixth syllable is considered a *settenàrio* even if an extra, unstressed eighth syllable is added or if the seventh syllable is not actually present. Similarly, an *endecasíllabo* has a stress on the tenth syllable, regardless whether the line actually has 10, 11 or 12 syllables.

The following example contains four typical *settenari* that are sung by Alfredo in the first act of Verdi's *La traviata*. The stressed sixth syllable is underscored in each line. The text continues a thought that was begun in the previous line with the verb *"vissi..."* (I have lived...)

...*Di quell'amor ch'è* <u>*L'a*</u>nima...	in that love which is the soul
Dell'universo in<u>te</u>ro	of the entire universe,
Misterïoso, al<u>te</u>ro,	mysterious, lofty,
Croce e delizia al <u>cor</u>.	torment and delight to my heart.

The first line has eight syllables, ending in a *parola sdrucciola*. The second and third lines have seven syllables each, ending in *parole piane*. The second line has a synalepha, *-so in-*, counted as one syllable. The third line has a semivowel that Verdi treated as a full vowel, which is the meaning of the double dot over the I of *misterïoso* (the word is pronounced in five syllables). There is also a synalepha, *-so al-*. The fourth line has two synalephas, *-ce e* and *-zia al*, and ends in a *parola tronca*, so it is only six syllables long.

The four lines of the example are all *settenari*, regardless of the actual syllable count (8, 7, 7, 6) and regardless of the fact that Alfredo repeats some words, singing more syllables than the librettist wrote.

Chapter 7 gives another example of syllable counting and detailed information about how to sing synalephas.

Capitalization in Italian Titles

In designing a program, one needs to know how to capitalize titles correctly in the various languages that will be sung. Printed music may have titles completely in upper-case, and different selections may come from publishers who followed different procedures. The singer needs to list the titles with a degree of uniformity and also respect the customs of the different languages.

In general, capitalization is used less in Italian than in English. Some publishers, for instance, use capitalization for the beginning of every line of poetry, while others do not. In the text of an aria, usually, capitalization is used only for the first word of each sentence.

When a title consists of several words, only the first word and proper names are capitalized (as also in French). It is not correct to capitalize all the words of a certain length, as in English. These are examples:

 Track 9

Le violette

'O sole mio

Il barbiere di Siviglia (*Siviglia* is a city, Seville)

Tu ch'hai le penne, Amore (*Amore* is the personification of love)

Chi m'ascolta il canto usato

Part 2: The Sounds of Italian

A Note About Part 2

Part 2 is arranged so that each Italian sound can be studied and practiced separately:

- Chapter 4 discusses the seven Italian vowels, arranged in order from bright vowels through dark ones, and the two semivowels.

- Chapter 5 discusses the 22 consonants, arranged according to their manner of articulation and then by the place of articulation.

- Chapter 6 discusses Italian diphthongs.

This logical order, corresponding to the numbered list of Italian phonemes on page 120, makes it easy to compare similar sounds, as well as to locate information for review .

There is an Alphabetical Key to Italian spellings on page 98.

Chapter 4: Vowels and Semivowels

The following chart shows how the seven Italian vowels relate to each other. Vowels that are spoken with a relatively smaller mouth space are on the line labeled Level I, and those with the mouth more open are farther down. Italian has no vowels in Level II, where English has /ɪ/, as in "lid," and /ʊ/, as in "put."

Vowels on the left side of the chart are formed primarily by raising the tongue and moving it forward in the mouth. Vowels on the right are formed by rounding the lips (or by lifting the body of the tongue). The "central" vowel uses little or none of either action.

Track 10

	Bright/ Tongue	Central	Dark/ Rounded Lips
Level I	/i/		/u/
Level II	none		none
Level III	/e/		/o/
Level IV	/ɛ/		/ɔ/
Level V		/a/	

Notice that certain common English vowels never occur in Italian at all. If you hear one of these vowels in your Italian, it is a mistake:

- /ɪ/ as in "kit,"

- /ʊ/ as in "push,"

- /æ/ as in "cat,"

- /ʌ/ as in "cup,"

- /ə/ as in "aside," and

- /ɝ/, the r-colored vowel in "turn."

The chart of the complete IPA on page 119 shows how these English vowels compare to Italian vowels.

Practicing Italian Vowels

An Italian vowel keeps its clear, pure sound no matter what other sound may come before it or after it. This is not true of English, where a vowel can become a neutral /ə/, like the final vowel of "operetta" /ɑpərɛtə/. An English vowel can become an unintended diphthong, as in English "Oh!" or "steel," or vanish altogether, as may happen in the second syllable of "cotton" /katn/. These things never happen to an Italian vowel.

All Italian vowels are correctly spoken with the tip of the tongue touching the inner surface of the lower teeth (the tongue leaves this position only briefly to articulate certain consonants). The jaw muscles are always relaxed, doing only the minimum to produce the correct degree of mouth opening.

The descriptions of the various vowels assume that the tip of the tongue is *always behind the lower teeth* and the jaw is *always as relaxed as possible.*

Bright Vowels

Emotionally, we react to certain vowel qualities and call them "bright." We may associate these sounds with happy or excited feelings. Acoustically, each of the bright vowels has a strong high overtone frequency that is weak or lacking in the vowels we call "dark." Physically, we produce the bright vowels by moving the tongue forward and up to whatever position produces the sound we want.

In all three bright vowels the body of the tongue rises and moves forward in the mouth, while the tip of the tongue stays behind the lower teeth. The position of the lips is less important; we often associate the bright vowels with smiling, but the lips may be either smiling or relaxed. If the lips are even slightly rounded, the vocal quality is somewhat darkened.

1. /i/, LOWER-CASE I   *Bright, Level I vowel*
Articulation
The blade of the tongue is raised and brought forward to form a narrow space between it and the upper teeth. The sides of the tongue gently touch the upper molars and the tongue forms a channel through which the breath passes. The lips are either relaxed or smiling.

Comparison
Italian /i/ is the same as the English vowel in "seen." The most common error is to substitute an English "short I" /ɪ/, a sound that does not exist in Italian. This is likely to happen in words that are similar in both languages, e.g., *invento* (I invent).

In English we never say a pure /i/ before R; instead, we substitute the diphthong /ɪə/, as in "fear." Also /i/ before L is usually spoken as /iəl/. Italian /i/ remains pure, regardless of what consonants precede or follow. To achieve this, hold the vowel as long as possible before letting the tongue move quickly to the consonant.

Be especially sure to avoid the sound of /ɪ/ in unstressed syllables. Ironically, when we say the phrase "in Italian," we are using vowels that do not exist in the Italian language.

 Track 11

Spellings:
I, Í (and J, an obsolete spelling found in old texts)

il vino, i vini	/viːno viːni/	wine, wines
il limite, i limiti	/liːmite liːmiti/	limit, limits
salí	/sali/	he/she/it climbed
avversarj (obsolete)	/avːversaːri/	adversaries

Be careful that I keeps its pure sound before L, N and R and does not take on the English sounds that are heard in words like "bill," "in" or "mere."

l'illusione	/lil:luzjo̱:ne/	illusion
insiste	/ins i̱ste/	he/she insists
i mirtilli	/mirti̱l:li/	blueberries
irreale	/ir:rea̱:le/	unreal

A few verb forms end in -II. When time permits, the second /i/ might be articulated with a breath impulse, but at most tempos only one /i:/ will be sung.

udii	/udi̱:i/	I heard

Before another vowel, the letter I can have three different functions, as in these three words, each which ends in -IA: *follia, gloria, caccia.* In *follia* the stressed syllable is *-li-*, containing the long pure vowel /i:/.

la follia	/fol:li̱:a/	folly

In *gloria* the stressed syllable is *glo-*, and the I is a semivowel /j/, as described later in this chapter.

la gloria	/glo̱:rja/	glory

In *caccia* the letter I is not pronounced at all; it is present only to alter the consonant to its soft form, as described in Chapter 5.

la caccia	/kat:tʃa/	hunting

These three words illustrate one of the few confusing difficulties in Italian (few compared to English, which has so many). Make use of a good dictionary when you are not absolutely sure how to treat the combination of I and another vowel.

Guarini,[1] G. Caccini: *Amarilli, mia bella,* mm. 22–27.
From *26 Italian Songs and Arias*, Alfred Publishing Co., Inc., p. 9.

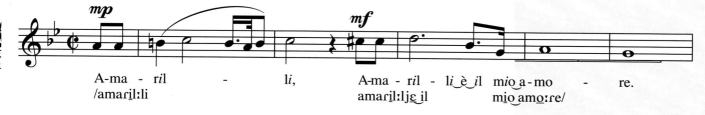

A-ma - ril - li,　　A-ma - ril - li è il mio a-mo - re.
/amari̱l:li　　amari̱l:ljɛ il　　mi̱o amo̱:re/

(Amaryllis is my love.)

---

[1]In the identification of musical examples, the poet's name is given before the composer's name, if it is known. If it is unknown or if the composer wrote the words, only one name is given.

2. /e/, LOWER CASE E   *Bright, Level III vowel*

Articulation

The blade of the tongue is raised and brought forward almost as much as for /i/. The sides touch the upper molars so that the tongue forms a channel somewhat wider than for /i/. The lips are either relaxed or smiling.

Comparison

Italian /e/ resembles the English vowel in "say," but /e/ is never pronounced as a diphthong. The pure vowel in Italian *se* (if) contrasts with the diphthong in English "say" /sɛɪ/.

To learn the pure /e/ of Italian, sing the vowel on a single prolonged tone. Let the jaw and tongue remain motionless both at the beginning and the end of the tone. Next, practice starting and stopping the tone repeatedly without any movement in the jaw or tongue. Any change of position will cause an unwanted diphthong.

Italians call this vowel *e chiuso* /ɛkːkjuːzo/ (closed E) in contrast to "open E," which is described next. It requires lifting and moving the tongue forward to a degree that may seem unfamiliar and unnatural to an English speaker. The /e/ in French (*café*) and German (*leben*) is even higher and more closed.

Following English spelling rules we expect to say short, open vowels before double consonants: for instance, "banner" and "bitter" have short, open vowels, in contrast to longer, more closed vowels in "bane" and "bite." There is no such rule in Italian: *e chiuso* occurs in many words before a double consonant, as shown in examples below. In such cases, *e chiuso* is short, but still closed. It is a common error for an English speaker to mispronounce such words as a result of applying an English rule to Italian spelling.

Spelling: E, É

e	/e/	and
la pena, le pene	/peːna peːne/	pain, pains
la mela, le mele	/meːla meːle/	apple, apples
temerete	/temereːte/	you (pl.) will fear
perché	/perke/	because
la carezza	/karetːtsa/	caress
potremmo	/potremːmo/	if we could

Rossi: *Anime voi,* mm. 4–6.
From *Gateway to Italian Art Songs*, page 9.

cre - de - te a   me,— cre - de - te   che quel   mal   che v'ac - co - ra
/kredeːte a   me   kredeːte   ke kwel   mal   ke vakːkɔːra/

(Believe me, believe, that the evil that afflicts you....)

3. /ɛ/, Epsilon

Bright, Level IV vowel

Articulation
The tongue is brought forward, but raised much less than for /e/. The sides of the tongue touch the upper molars lightly or not at all. The lips are relaxed or smiling, and the jaw is almost as open as for /a/.

Comparison
Italian /ɛ/ has a slightly higher tongue position, and is therefore a little brighter, than the English vowel in "red."

In English /ɛ/ is always short and is never final in a word. In Italian it may be either short or long, and it may be final. As singers, we must be able to prolong it in music without changing it to a diphthong.

Italians call this vowel *e aperto* /ɛ apɛrto/ (open E) in contrast to "closed E," which was described above.

Track 13

Spelling: E in some stressed syllables, È.

è	/ɛ/	is
mesto, -a	/mɛsto mɛsta/	sad
bene	/bɛːne/	well, beloved
leggo	/lɛgːgo/	I read

In spoken Italian /ɛ/ occurs only in stressed syllables. Therefore:

Rule #1: E in unstressed syllables is always /e/ in spoken Italian.

Rule #2: E in stressed syllables can be either /e/ or /ɛ/.

Corollary: Because there is only one main stress in a word, there can be only one /ɛ/. Other E's in the same word are all /e/.

Italian spelling does not indicate whether to say /e/ or /ɛ/ in a stressed syllable. Some rules exist, but they are difficult to apply and prone to exceptions. If they were introduced here, they would occupy many pages of text and take on more importance than they deserve. The distinction between /e/ and /ɛ/ must be made, but the most practical way to deal with it is to use a dictionary and check every stressed E. (For those who want more detail, typical cases and useful words are found in a supplement beginning on page 101.)

In English, E before a double consonant is pronounced /ɛ/, but this rule does not apply to Italian. E before a double consonant can be either closed or open.

If your dictionary gives only the infinitive form of verbs, be aware that the conjugated forms may have different vowel qualities because the stress is shifted.

| temere, temo | /temeːre tɛːmo/ | to fear, I fear |
| sentire, sento | /sentiːre sɛnto/ | to hear, I hear |

Phonetic symbols for open E /ɛ/ and open O /ɔ/ are not used in ordinary Italian printing, but they have been used in many American textbooks to help students memorize the correct pronunciation of common words. That is why the symbols are used in Italian texts throughout the Alfred Vocal Masterworks Series.

Some singers, preferring the open quality, intentionally use /ɛ/ in unstressed syllables. Some singers use /ɛ/ in unstressed syllables, but only after the stressed syllable of the word and not before it. These preferences are personal, stylistic choices that may or may not be right for your voice. They are not observed in this book. Follow your teacher's advice.

Similarly, notice what happens to the open E of the word *bello* when suffixes shift the stress. (The vowel is still short, but it is closed.)

bello	/bɛl:lo/	beautiful
abbellisco	/ab:bel:lisko/	I am beautifying
Bellini	/bel:li:ni/	composer's name
la bellezza	/bel:let:tsa/	beauty

Finally, after all of the above has been said, one must admit that in daily speech /e/ and /ɛ/ may be difficult for foreigners to distinguish by ear. But Italians distinguish clearly between the sounds in their minds, and the difference cannot be ignored in artistic singing.

A. Scarlatti: *Alfin m'ucciderete,* mm. 36–37.
From *Gateway to Italian Art Songs,* page 26.

Io mo - ri - rei con-ten - to....
/io moɾiɾɛi   kontɛnto/

(I would die happy....)

The Central Vowel

The central vowel uses neither forward lifting of the tongue nor lip rounding.

4. /a/, LOWER-CASE A   *Central, Level V vowel*

Articulation
The jaw is lower than for any other vowel. The tongue is slightly arched forward, and the sides of the tongue may not touch the upper molars at all. The lips are relaxed or smiling.

Comparison
Italian /a/ is the vowel color heard at the beginning of the diphthong that we call "long I," as in "aisle" or "ice." It is not the same as the dark AH /ɑ/ heard in "father." In English the brighter vowel is heard only as an element in a diphthong and in some regional dialects.

The bright /a/ is universally spoken in Italian, but some singers intentionally darken the vowel as a personal preference. (Many singers modify vowels for both technical and aesthetic reasons. Such personal decisions should be made between the singer and the voice teacher, and they are not discussed in this book.)

In English an unstressed A does not keep the pure sound of /a/, but changes to the neutral sound /ə/ heard at the end of "sofa." Take special care that Italian /a/ keeps its pure sound in unstressed syllables.

Spelling: A, À   Track 14

santa	/sa̲nta/	holy; (female) saint
basta!	/ba̲sta/	enough!
la cantata	/kanta̲ːta/	cantata
avanzata	/avantsa̲ːta/	advanced; far along
avrà	/avra̲/	he/she/it will have

Conti: *Dopo tante e tante pene*, mm. 40–43.
From *Gateway to Italian Art Songs*, page 44.

Quel - la_____   fiam - ma_____   che   m'ac   -   cen - de....
/kwe̲ːla   fjam̲ːma   ke   matːt ʃɛnde/

(That flame that enflames me...)

Dark Vowels

Emotionally, we react to certain vowel qualities and call them "dark." We may associate these sounds with somber or serious feelings. Acoustically, the dark vowels are formed by low partials; they lack the strong high overtones that characterize bright vowels. Physically, we produce the dark vowels by rounding the lips to whatever opening size produces the sound we want or by lifting and shaping the tongue without moving it forward. Fine Italian singers use lip rounding for these vowels.

Rounding the dark vowels may feel unfamiliar to you. Many North Americans say dark vowels with no lip rounding at all, instead shaping the vowel with the tongue more or less tense and high in the back of the mouth.

Lip rounding can be done with very little muscular activity by bringing in the corners of the mouth toward the center line. Use a mirror for practice. The correct position may feel unfamiliar, but it is advisable for singing Italian easily and expressively. With the lips rounded properly, your tongue can remain lower in the mouth and more relaxed, benefitting your tone. In all of the dark vowels the tip of the tongue remains behind the lower teeth and the body of the tongue remains as relaxed as possible near the center of the mouth.

Books about speech typically contain charts that show the tongue humped in the back of the mouth for the dark vowels. This author believes that most such charts are misleading and that even the few accurate X-ray views that exist are more relevant to speech than to singing. In singing, one can pronounce the dark vowels with a much larger space above the tongue than one would use in ordinary speech.

5. /u/, LOWER-CASE U   *Dark, Level I vowel*

Articulation
The corners of the mouth are actively pulled inward toward the center line of the mouth, so that the lips are more rounded than for any other vowel and slightly protruded. The body of the tongue may rise somewhat but in as relaxed a way as possible. The relaxed jaw is relatively closed.

Comparison
Italian /u/ resembles the English vowel in "truth," spoken with a degree of lip rounding that will seem exaggerated to most North Americans. Use a mirror to practice this vowel. The circle formed by the lips has about the same diameter as an ordinary pencil, although more opening is needed for higher pitches.

In Italian the letter U by itself is always pronounced with a pure /u/. The /ju/ sound heard in English "music" or "pew" is spelled IU in Italian.

Track 15 **Spelling**: U, Ú

la luna	/luːna/	moon
subito	/suːbito/	suddenly
utile	/uːtile/	useful
la virtú	/virtu/	virtue

Be careful that U keeps its pure sound before L, N and R and does not take on the English sounds that are heard in words like "full," "fun" or "fur."

ultimo, -a	/<u>u</u>ltimo <u>u</u>ltima/	last
il punto	/p<u>u</u>nto/	dot, period
turbato	/turb<u>a</u>:to/	disturbed
l'urlo	/<u>u</u>rlo/	shout

NOTE: U is sometimes a semivowel /w/, described later in this chapter.

Metastasio, Bellini: *Per pietà, bell'idol mio,* mm. 46–48.
From *Gateway to Italian Art Songs,* page 125.

Se	mi	stru*g* - go	a'	tuoi	bei	lu	-	mi....
/se	mi	stru<u>g</u>:go	a	tw<u>ɔ</u>i b<u>ɛ</u>i	lu:mi/		

(If I melt for your beautiful eyes....)

6. /o/, Lower-case O   *Dark, Level III vowel*

Articulation
The corners of the mouth are actively pulled inward toward the center line of the mouth, so that the lips are rounded (a little less than for /u/) and slightly protruded. The body of the tongue is as relaxed as possible. The jaw is relaxed in a half closed position.

Comparison
Italian /o/ resembles the English vowel in "rose," but Italian /o/ is more closed and is never pronounced as a diphthong. The pure vowel in Italian *lo* (the) contrasts with the diphthong in English "low" /loʊ/.

To learn the pure Italian /o/, try singing it on a prolonged single tone. Let the jaw, lips and tongue remain motionless both at the beginning and the end of the tone. Next, practice starting and stopping the tone repeatedly without any movement in the articulators. Any change of position will cause an unwanted diphthong.

> British and European pronouncing dictionaries may give a different pronunciation for the "long O:" not /oʊ/, but /əʊ/. For this diphthong, the tongue is raised forward to a position near the French *eu* or the German *ö*. It is used in some British dialects but not in the U.S. or Canada.

Italians call this vowel *o chiuso* /ɔk:kju:zo/ (closed O) in contrast to "open O," which is described next. It requires a rounding and darkening of the tone that may seem unfamiliar and unnatural to an English speaker. The /o/ in French (*l'eau*) and German (*ohne*) is rounded and darkened even more.

Track 16

Following English spelling rules, we expect to say short, open vowels before double consonants: for instance, "bottle" and "butter" have short, open vowels in contrast to longer, more closed vowels in "voter" and "boot." There is no such rule in Italian: *o chiuso* occurs in many words before a double consonant, as shown in examples below. In such cases, *o chiuso* is short, but still closed. It is a common error for an English speaker to mispronounce such words as a result of applying an English rule to Italian spelling.

Spelling: O

solo, -a	/so:lo so:la/	alone
molto	/molto/	much
conosco	/konosko/	I know
la bocca	/bok:ka/	mouth
la colpa	/kolpa/	guilt

Be careful that O keeps its pure quality in unstressed syllables and does not turn into the English vowels we hear in "color," "congress" or "chorus," all of which are different from each other.

il colore	/kolo:re/	color
contento	/kontɛnto/	satisfied, glad
il corista	/korista/	chorus singer

Bellini: *Vaga luna, che inargenti*, mm. 41–43.
From *Gateway to Italian Art Songs*, page 130.

| Con - to | l'o - re del | do - | lor.... |
| /konto | lo:re del | dolor/ | |

(I count the hours of sadness....)

7. /ɔ/, OPEN O   *Dark, Level IV vowel*

Articulation
The corners of the mouth are slightly pulled in toward the center line; the lip rounding is almost as narrow as for /o/, but a low jaw position makes the opening a vertical oval rather than a circle. The tongue is as relaxed and as flat as possible. The jaw is almost as open as for /a/.

Comparison
Some speakers of English use /ɔ/ regularly in words such as "ought, law, hall," but millions of others do not. If you habitually use the same vowel sound in "sock" and "saw," or in "cot" and "caught," it may be that the /ɔ/ vowel does not exist in your local speech. Even so, you probably use /ɔ/ as the first part of the diphthong in "joy," and you can learn to use it as an independent, pure vowel.

Track 17

Italians call this vowel *o aperto* /ɔ apɛrto/ (open O) in contrast to "closed O," which was described above.

Spelling: O in some stressed syllables, Ò

ho	/ɔ/	I have
poco, -a	/pɔ:ko pɔ:ka/	little
la volta	/vɔlta/	time; vault
avrò	/avrɔ/	I shall have
la coorte	/ko.ɔrte/	cohort

In spoken Italian /ɔ/ occurs only in stressed syllables. Therefore:

Rule #1: O in unstressed syllables is always /o/ in spoken Italian.

Rule #2: O in stressed syllables can be either /o/ or /ɔ/.

Corollary: Because there is only one main stress in a word, there can be only one /ɔ/. Other O's in the same word are all /o/.

Italian spelling does not indicate whether to say /o/ or /ɔ/ in stressed syllables. Some rules exist, but they are difficult to apply and prone to exceptions. If they were introduced here, they would occupy many pages and they would take on more importance than they deserve. The distinction between /o/ and /ɔ/ must be made, but the most practical way to deal with it is to use a dictionary and check every stressed O. (For those who want more detail, typical cases and useful words are found in a supplement beginning on page 104.)

> Some singers, preferring the open quality, intentionally use /ɔ/ in unstressed syllables. Some singers use /ɔ/ in unstressed syllables, but only after the stressed syllable of the word and not before it. These preferences are personal, stylistic choices that may or may not be right for your voice. They are not observed in this book. Follow your teacher's advice.

If your dictionary gives only the infinitive form of verbs, be aware that the conjugated forms may have different vowel qualities because the stress is shifted.

scoprire, scopro   /skopriːre skɔːpro/   to discover, I discover

Similarly, notice what happens to the open O of the word *occhio* when suffixes shift the stress. (The vowel is still short, but it is closed.)

occhio	/ɔkːkjo/	eye
adocchiare	/adokːkjaːre/	to catch sight of
gli occhiali	/okːkjaːli/	eyeglasses

Finally, after all of the above has been said, one must admit that in daily speech /o/ and /ɔ/ may be difficult for foreigners to distinguish by ear. But Italians distinguish clearly between the sounds in their minds, and the difference cannot be ignored in artistic singing.

Goethe, Verdi: *Deh, pietoso, oh Addolorata,* mm. 6–10.
From *Gateway to Italian Art Songs,* page 153.

U-na spa - da fit-ta_in co - re, vol-gi gl'oc - chi,___ de - so - la - ta,...
/uːna spaːda fitːta_in kɔːre vɔldʒi ʎːʎɔkːki dezolaːta/

(With a sword piercing your heart, you turn your eyes, desolate woman,...)

Semivowels

Semivowels are sounds that begin in one vowel position and move to another vowel position so quickly that the first vowel is heard as if it were a kind of consonant. We do not call them vowels because they are not able to form the nucleus of a syllable.

Semivowels are sometimes called semiconsonants because they can start syllables, but they do not stop or obstruct the breath flow. The articulators that form the semivowels are in such close proximity that if they were any closer, the breath would be stopped or disturbed, and so phoneticians call them approximants.

In school children learn that in English W is a consonant and Y can be either a vowel or a consonant. More accurately, W and Y are not consonants because they do not interfere with the breath stream; they are semivowels. Italian has the same two semivowels as English; instead of W and Y, Italian uses I and U.

A semivowel normally occurs in Italian when I or U is followed by another vowel in the same syllable. You may need help from a dictionary in identifying these situations, however, because in some words I or U is not a semivowel, but the first vowel of a diphthong (as described in Chapter 6). Furthermore, I is silent in the digraphs CI, GI, GLI or SCI before another vowel (as described in Chapter 5).

8. /j/, LOWER-CASE J   *Bright semivowel*

Articulation
The sound begins with the tongue raised to the position of /i/, but the tongue moves immediately to the position of whatever vowel follows.

Comparison
Italian /j/ is exactly the same as the first sound in "you," except that English speakers sometimes start it from /ɪ/ instead of starting precisely from /i/, as Italians do. Italian does not contain the combination /ji/, as in English "yield."

Spellings: I, unstressed, before A, E, O or U.

piano	/pja̱ːno/	softly
pieno, -a	/pjɛ̱ːno pjɛ̱ːna/	full
piove	/pjɔ̱ːve/	it's raining
più	/pju̱/	more

J, in proper names and in old editions.

gioja, gioia	/dʒɔ̱ːja/	joy
ajuto, aiuto	/aju̱ːto/	help
Jacopo, Iacopo	/ja̱ːkopo/	Jacob

Exceptions:

- Silent I, spelled CI, GI, GLI or SCI before another vowel discussed in Chapter 5).

- Stressed I in diphthongs (discussed in Chapter 6).

- Unstressed I in a prefix that precedes a vowel, such as *ri-*.

riamare   /ri.amaːɾe/   to love in return

Concerning other exceptions, see the paragraph following discussion of /w/.

Errico, Tosti: *Ideale,* mm. 12 –16.
From *Gateway to Italian Art Songs*, page 182.

ne   l'a - *ria*, nel pro-fu - mo de*i*   fio - ri;   e   fu   p*ie* - na   la stan-za so - *li* - ta - *ria*

/nelːlaɾja   nel profuːmo   dɛi   fjoːɾi   e   fu   pjɛːna   la stantsa solitaːrja/

(...in the air, in the perfume of flowers, and the solitary room was full...)

9. /w/, LOWER-CASE W   *Dark semivowel*

Articulation
The sound begins with the lips rounded to the position of /u/, but they move immediately to the position of whatever vowel follows.

Comparison
Italian /w/ is exactly the same as the first sound in "way." Italian does not contain the combination /wu/, as in English "woo." UU never occurs.

Notice that Italian U is never silent, as it is in French *quel* and Spanish *que*.

Track 19

Spelling: U, unstressed before A, E, I or O (except after L or R).

la guardia	/gwaɾdja/	guard
la guerra	/gwɛrːra/	war
la guida	/gwiːda/	guidance
questa	/kwesta/	this
uomo, uomini	/wɔːmo wɔːmini/	man, men

Exception:
- Stressed U in diphthongs (discussed in Chapter 6).

Vittorelli, Verdi: *In solitaria stanza,* mm. 22 –26.
From *Gateway to Italian Art Songs*, page 146.

...e   gri - do in suon   che   p*uo* - te   le   ru - pi   in-te - ne - rir.

/e   griːdo in   swɔn   ke   pwɔːte   le   ruːpi   intenerir/

(....and I cry out with a sound that would soften rocky cliffs.)

Further Notes About Semivowels

Track 20

Pronouncing dictionaries show a few cases in which, after L or R, an unstressed I or U forms a short, separate syllable. Composers usually treat these cases as semivowels. For example, Canepari spells the name Liú phonetically in two syllables, /liu̯/, but in the aria, *"Signore, ascolta!"* from Puccini's *Turandot,* the servant girl Liú sings her own name on a single note. This shows that Puccini expected the name to be sung as one syllable, /lju/.

A few words contain both semivowels /wj/, forming one syllable with the following vowel:

quieto	/kwjɛ:to/	quiet
acquietare	/ak:kwjeta:re/	to ease, appease
seguiate	/segwja:te/	you (pl.) may follow

Chapter 5: Consonants

English and Italian have roughly the same number of consonant phonemes, but they function quite differently. Clusters of consecutive consonants are much more common in English than in Italian, partly because most English words end in consonants, while most Italian words end in vowels.

Dramatic singing in English, delivered with expressive energy before a live audience, requires strong consonants and a great deal of breath energy. The drama of Italian singing comes more through vowels than consonants, and yet the consonants must be audible and expressive. Single Italian consonants are light and quick, taking less breath energy than in English. Double consonants are an important feature of expressive Italian, especially if they are voiced.

Italian Consonant Phonemes

Consonants are presented in this chapter in the same numerical order as in the list of Italian phonemes (page 120), part of which is repeated here, beginning with phoneme 10. (The first nine phonemes are the seven vowels and two semivowels.) They appear in this order: nasals; laterals; trills; stops; fricatives; affricates. Within each group consonants are arranged by their point of articulation in the mouth, from front to back.

IPA Symbols	Names of Symbols	Similar English Sounds
10. /m/	Lower-case M	mime
11. /n/	Lower-case N	noon
12. /ɲ/	Left-tail N	Spanish *señor* (none in English)
13. /ŋ/	Eng	sing
14. /l/	Lower-case L	laugh
15. /ʎ/	Turned Y	(none in English)
16. /r/	Lower-case R	(trill R, none in English)
or /ɾ/	Fish-hook R	merry (formal, tap R)
17. /p/	Lower-case P	pie
18. /b/	Lower-case B	buy
19. /t/	Lower-case T	too
20. /d/	Lower-case D	do
21. /k/	Lower-case K	cap
22. /g/	Lower-case G	gap
23. /f/	Lower-case F	fat
24. /v/	Lower-case V	vat
25. /s/	Lower-case S	Sue
26. /z/	Lower-case Z	zoo
27. /ʃ/	Esh	shoe
28. /ts/	T-S affricate	sits up
29. /dz/	D-Z affricate	adds on
30. /tʃ/	T-Esh affricate	chin
31. /dʒ/	D-Yogh affricate	gym

Silent Letters

Every letter in an Italian word must be pronounced, with only two exceptions.

(1) H is always silent in Italian, as it is in French and Spanish and in some English words, such as "honor" and "hour."

H is used (aside from foreign words):
• to harden certain consonants, described as the next topic;

• in some exclamations, such as:

Track 21

    oh!, ahi!, ahimè!   /o ai aimɛ/   oh!, alas!

• in obsolete spellings found in very old music, such as:

    honore (obs.), onore   /ono̲ːɾe/   honor

• in four forms of the verb *avere* (to have). (In a phrase, the preceding vowel or consonant forms a new syllable with the vowel of the verb.)

ho, non ho	/ɔ no.nɔ̲/	I have, I don't have
hai, che cos'hai?	/a̲i ke ko.za̲i/	you have, what's wrong with you?
ha, egli ha	/a eʎːʎa̲/	he has, he has
hanno, han (truncated)	/a̲nːno an/	they have

(2) I is silent when it is used to soften certain consonants, described in the next paragraph.

Soft and Hard Pronunciations

The letters C, G and SC follow a set of rules that distinguish between so-called hard and soft pronunciations. It is easier to learn about them by understanding the pattern they follow before studying them separately. (All Romance languages have special rules for these letters, but with different results.) Detailed discussions about the sounds are found on the pages listed at the right.

Track 22

C, G and SC have their soft sounds before the vowels E and I.

ce, ci	/tʃe tʃi/	Page 72
ge, gi	/dʒe dʒi/	Page 73
sce, sci	/ʃe ʃi/	Page 69

C, G and SC have their hard sounds before A, O, U or consonants.

ca, co, cu, cra	/ka ko ku kra/	Page 63
ga, go, gu, gra	/ga go gu gra/	Page 64
sca, sco, scu, scra	/ska sko sku skra/	Page 63

If a hard C, G or SC is desired before E or I, an H is used.

che, chi	/ke ki/	Page 63
ghe, ghi	/ge gi/	Page 65
sche, schi	/ske ski/	Page 63

If a soft C, G or SC is desired before A, O or U, an I is used

cia, cio, ciu	/tʃa tʃo tʃu/	Page 72
gia, gio, giu	/dʒa dʒo dʒu/	Page 73
scia, scio, sciu	/ʃa ʃo ʃu/	Page 69

Dentalization

Most English speakers articulate the sounds of D, L, N and T on the alveolar ridge, but Italian speakers articulate them on the inner surface of the upper teeth. This articulation brings the tongue noticeably farther forward in Italian than in English, with benefit to the vocal tone.

These four letters are easy to remember because they are the letters in "DeNTaL." IPA has a special dental diacritic /ˌ/, but we do not have to use it because the four dental consonants are always dentalized, without exception.

Lack of Aspiration

English and other Germanic languages use a burst of air, called aspiration, for the voiceless stop plosive consonants /k p t/. A narrow transcription shows aspiration as /kʰ pʰ tʰ/. In Italian and other Romance languages the stop plosives open gently and the vowel sound begins immediately, without aspiration. Often, a voiceless stop consonant is nearly soundless; it is recognized more by the way the vowel begins than by its own sound.

Consonant Clusters

After the discussion of each consonant, there is a list of the possible clusters that include it. Most of them are familiar to an English speaker, but some require practice. The examples include all of the combinations of consonants and semivowels that are likely to occur in singing Italian. Not included are consonant combinations that occur in modern loan words.

Examples of clusters are given under the first phoneme in the cluster; for instance, *placido* is listed under /p/ but not under /l/.

Geminated Consonants

For our Italian to sound authentic, we have to pay particular attention to the contrast between single and GEMINATED (pronounced double) consonants. A single consonant between two vowels should be articulated as quickly as possible, taking the least possible time away from the vowels before and after. In contrast to the lightness of Italian single consonants, geminated consonants noticeably interrupt the flowing sequence of vowels in Italian singing.

To show gemination, dictionaries and most diction texts simply double the consonant symbol. In our IPA transcriptions we also add the lengthening symbol, like this: /mːm/. Even if it is superfluous, the lengthening symbol serves as a visual cue to remind us which words have geminated consonants and which do not, so that we learn to sing them correctly by habit.

These are examples of words that are distinguished only by the medial consonant being single or geminated.

 Track 23

la casa /kaːza/, house	la cassa /kasːsa/, case, chest
l'eco /ɛːko/, echo	ecco /ɛkːko/, here/there it is
il fato /faːto/, fate	il fatto /fatːto/, fact
il fumo /fuːmo/, smoke	fummo /fumːmo/, we were
nono /nɔːno/, ninth	il nonno /nɔnːno/, grandfather
il papa /paːpa/, pope	la pappa /papːpa/, baby food

English does not use geminated consonants within words. There is no audible difference, for example, between the M in "coming" and the MM in "humming," or between the N in "money" and the NN in "sunny." But we have gemination between two words if the same consonant ends one word and begins the next. Examples of such gemination in English are used throughout this chapter.

In singing, a geminated consonant takes time away from the preceding note. Various types of consonants behave in different ways in singing.

- Voiced consonants form what we call sung doubles. The first consonant is sung on the pitch of the preceding note and takes some of its value. The second is sung on the pitch of the next note, with a legato connection between them.

- Voiceless stop consonants form what we call STOPPED DOUBLES. The first consonant stops the preceding tone, taking some of its value. The second begins the next syllable as if it were a new attack. There is a silence between the syllables, not a legato connection.

- All other voiceless consonants form what we call SOUNDED DOUBLES. The first consonant sound takes some of the value of the preceding note. The second begins the following note as if it were a new attack. Between the syllables we hear a voiceless sound, not a vocal tone.

Nasal Consonants

English has three nasal consonants, but Italian has four. Although they are quieter than fully resonated vowel tones, they fit smoothly into a vocal line. Like all other voiced consonants, the nasals must be tuned carefully to the desired pitch.

10. /m/, LOWER-CASE M   *Voiced bilabial nasal*

Articulation: Both lips.
Lips: Closed gently.
Teeth: Slightly separated.
Tongue tip: Touching the lower incisors.
Tongue body: Shaped for the neighboring vowel (not touching the palate).
Air flow: Through the nose only.
Resonation: In the mouth space over the tongue and in the nose.

Comparison
English and Italian /m/ are the same.

Gemination
MM /m:m/ is a sung double. As in the expression "some more," the lips close for the first M. Vocal tone continues until the second M opens to a vowel. If the two syllables are on different pitches, the consonant is sung on both.

M at the end of a syllable is lengthened almost as if it were doubled, but this is not shown in IPA. See the second example in the following list.

Spelling: M, MM.

la musica	/muːzika/	music
l'ombra	/ombra/	shadow
andiam!	/andjam/	let's go!
la commedia	/komːmɛːdja/	comedy
dimmi	/dimːmi/	tell me

Clusters: /mj/, /mw/. See /zm/.

l'accademia	/akːkadɛːmja/	academy
muovo	/mwɔːvo/	I am moving

Leoncavallo: *Mattinata*, mm. 15–17.
From *Gateway to Italian Art Songs*, page 188.

Com - mos - so da un fre - mi - to ar - ca - no...
/komːmɔsːso   da un frɛːmito arkaːno/

(Moved by a mysterious shudder....)

11. /n/, LOWER-CASE N

Voiced dental nasal

Articulation: Tongue touching all of the upper teeth.
Lips: Open.
Teeth: Slightly separated.
Tongue tip: Touching the back of the upper incisors. (The under side of the tongue may be seen in a mirror.)
Tongue body: Relaxed, with the sides raised to contact all of the upper teeth.
Air flow: Through the nose only.
Resonation: In the mouth space over the tongue and in the nose.

Comparison

English /n/ is formed on the alveolar ridge, slightly back from the Italian /n/. The forward tongue position for Italian /n/ is beneficial for vocal production.

Notice that in English we normally let the jaw close every time the tongue rises. Italians let the tongue rise independently and articulate /n/ without help from the jaw. This saves effort and allows the vowels that occur before and after /n/ to have a pure tone color. If the tongue and jaw are independent from each other, words with /n/ can be sung more easily on high tones.

In order to gain independence of the tongue, practice syllables with /n/ while holding one hand on your cheek; the jaw need not move at all.

Gemination

NN /nːn/ is a sung double. As in the expression "fine name," a closure is made for the first N. Vocal tone continues until the second N opens to a vowel. If the two syllables are on different pitches, the consonant is sung on both.

N at the end of a syllable is lengthened almost as if it were doubled, but this is not shown in IPA. See the third word in the following list.

Spelling: N, NN. Track 25

no!	/nɔ/	no!
fino	/fiːno/	fine
andante	/andante/	going, walking
Anna	/anːna/	Anna
donnesco	/donːnesko/	ladylike

Clusters: /nj/, /nw/. See /zn/.

finiamo	/finjaːmo/	let's finish
nuovo	/nwɔːvo/	new

Special Note About N

In spoken Italian, allophones often replace /n/ before another consonant:

Before P or B, N becomes bilabial /m/.
Before F or V, N becomes labiodental /ɱ/.
Before GN, N becomes postalveolar /ɲ/.
Before hard C or hard G, N becomes palatal /ŋ/.
Before T or D, N naturally remains dental /n/.

Therefore, the word *con* (with) may be pronounced five different ways in the phrases: *con Paola, con Virginia, con gnocchi, con Carlo, con Tonio.* (Canepàri, *Manuale*, p. 75).

Even native speakers of Italian disagree about using these allophones in singing. There is majority agreement on one: /ŋ/, which is consonant 13 in this book. But the others may also be useful, especially for a comic or conversational effect.

Dr. Paolo Zedda, University of Lyon, France, a native Italian singer and singing teacher, kindly read and commented on the manuscript of this book. He argued vigorously that the /m/ and /ɱ/ allophones for N are a natural part of standard Italian and should be used in all singing. Perhaps his view will prevail if, as he says, Italians sing the way they speak and pay less heed to orthography.

Fucini, Puccini: *E l'uccellino,* mm. 4–7.
From *Gateway to Italian Art Songs*, page 202.

E   l'uc - cel - li - no   can - ta   sul - la   fron - da:
/elutːtʃelːliːno   kanta   sulla   fronda/

(And the little bird sings on the branch...)

12. /ɲ/, LEFT-TAIL N   *Voiced palatal nasal*

Articulation: Tongue blade and hard palate.
Lips: Open.
Teeth: Slightly separated.
Tongue tip: Touching the lower incisors (or pointing toward them).
Tongue blade: Raised, contacting the front part of the hard palate and the upper molars on the sides.
Air flow: Through the nose only.
Resonation: In the mouth space behind the raised tongue and in the nose.

Comparison
This sound is in French (*seigneur*) and Spanish (*cañón*), but not in English.

After /ɲ/, the tongue either moves to the /i/ position or passes through the /i/ position on the way to some other vowel. Because our ears are attuned to English sounds, we interpret this movement as the semivowel /j/. Italians do not hear it that way and do not use /j/ in transcribing it.

There is a slight, but distinct difference between /nj/ and /ɲ/, specifically in the tongue position. This is how to discover the Italian sound /ɲ/:

• Say the English words "on you" /ɑn ju/, and notice that the tip of the tongue strikes the alveolar ridge.
  • Now say the words again, with the tip of the tongue touching the lower teeth. The result will be the Italian syllables *agnu* /aɲːɲu/ (this is a made-up combination, not a word).

Gemination
Geminated /ɲːɲ/ is a sung double. GN is always geminated between two vowels (even in different words), and it seldom occurs any other way. The tongue rises to make the palatal contact at the end of the first syllable. Vocal tone continues until the tongue lowers again for the next vowel. If the two syllables are on different pitches, the consonant is sung on both.

 Spelling: GN.

uno gnocco	/unoɲːɲɔkːko/	potato-flour dumpling
la lasagna	/lazaɲːɲa/	a form of pasta
il segno	/seɲːɲo/	sign
ogni	/oɲːɲi/	every
ognuno	/oɲːɲuːno/	everyone

GNI is also found in some verb forms where the I is considered silent.

segniamo	/seɲːɲaːmo/	we are marking
bagniate	/baɲːɲaːte/	you (pl) may swim

There are no clusters with /ɲ/.

Leoncavallo: *Lasciati amar,* mm. 35–36.
From *Gateway to Italian Art Songs*, page 192.

Dal   so - *gn*o tuo   no - vel - lo____
/dal   soɲːɲo tuo   novɛlːlo/

(From your new dream....)

13. /ŋ/, ENG

Voiced velar nasal

Articulation: Tongue body and palate.
Lips: Open.
Teeth: Separated.
Tongue tip: Touching the lower incisors.
Tongue body: Contacting the upper rear molars and the hard palate
(after bright vowels) or the soft palate (after dark vowels).
Air flow: Through the nose only.
Resonation: In the oral pharynx and in the nose.

Comparison

English and Italian /ŋ/ sound exactly the same.

English /ŋ/ is phonemic, as shown by minimum pairs, such as: "thin-thing."
Italian /ŋ/ is not phonemic, rather it is an allophone of /n/. Because /ŋ/ is an
allophone, Italian dictionaries ignore it and show /n/ instead. Nevertheless,
most singers and coaches recommend its use.

Just as with /n/, the tongue can form /ŋ/ without closing the jaw. And just as
singers may move the tongue forward to articulate /k/ and /g/ on the hard palate,
Italian /ŋ/ may also be pronounced farther forward in singing than in speech.

Gemination

Italian /ŋ/ cannot be doubled, but is pronounced nearly as long as a double
consonant. This is not shown in IPA.

Spelling: N before the sounds of /k/ or /g/, in a word or between two words.   *(Track 27)*

ancora	/aŋko:ra/	again
il sangue	/saŋgwe/	blood
languisce	/laŋgwiʃ:ʃe/	languishes
l'inquisitore	/iŋkwizito:re/	inquisitor
con Carlo	/koŋkarlo/	with Carlo
un guanto	/uŋgwanto/	a glove

There are no clusters with /ŋ/.

Francesca Caccini: *Che t'ho fatt'io,* mm. 25–30.
From *Italian Arias of the Baroque and Classical Eras,*
Alfred Publishing Co., Inc., page 20.

...In - gra - to se - no, già non vo - ler ch'io ven - ga me - no.
/iŋgra:to se:no dʒa non voler kio vɛŋga me:no/

(... ungrateful bosom, just do not wish for me to die.)

Lateral Consonants

Lateral consonants are formed when the breath passes around the raised tongue and escapes from the sides of the mouth. English has only one lateral consonant, but Italian has two.

Laterals are voiced and are nearly as resonant as vowels. Like the nasals, the laterals fit smoothly into a vocal line and must be in tune with the desired pitch.

14. /l/, LOWER-CASE L   *Voiced dental lateral approximant*

Articulation: Tongue tip and upper incisors.
Teeth: Separated.
Tongue tip: Touching the back of the upper incisors.
Tongue body: Narrow, avoiding contact with the teeth at the sides.
Air flow: Through the mouth, on both sides of the tongue.

Comparison
English /l/ is alveolar, that is, the apex of the tongue contacts the alveolar ridge, not the teeth. Italian /l/ is typically farther forward, which is favorable for singing.

"La-la-la" is a favorite refrain for folk songs in many languages, and it may have originated in Italy. One of the most singable consonants, /l/ can be sung on any pitch in one's range and fits easily into a legato line.

Some English speakers habitually pronounce a "dark L," with the tongue pulled back to the postalveolar area or even with the tip turned back (retroflex L). By contrast, Italians speak a "clear L" with the tongue much farther forward and the tip narrow, so that it feels pointed.

Italians let the tongue rise to articulate /l/ without closing the jaw. This reduces effort, makes high tones with /l/ easier, and allows the vowels that occur before and after /l/ to have a pure tone color. Practice "la-la-la" with a mirror or with one hand on your cheek, letting the jaw remain perfectly still.

Gemination
LL /lːl/ is a sung double. As in the phrase "until light," the tongue rises for the first L. Vocal tone continues until the second L opens to a vowel. If the two syllables are on different pitches, the consonant is sung on both.

L at the end of a syllable is lengthened nearly as much as if it were doubled, but this is not shown in IPA.

Track 28 **Spellings:** L, LL.

l'amore	/lamoːre/	love
il velo	/veːlo/	veil
il colpo mortal	/kɔlpo mortal/	fatal blow
il ballo	/balːlo/	dance, ball

Notice that the spelling -GLI- stands for consonant 15.

Clusters: /lj/, /lw/. Also see /bl/,/fl/, /gl/, /kl/, /pl/, /zl/.

| il sollievo | /sol:lj<u>ɛ</u>:vo/ | relief |
| il luogo | /il:lw<u>ɔ</u>:go/ | place |

Metastasio, Colbran-Rossini: *Già la notte s'avvicina,* mm. 4–8.
From *Gateway to Italian Art Songs*, page 80.

...de*l* - *la*   p*l*a - ci - da   ma - ri - na   *le*⸏   fre - sch'au - re_a re - spi - rar.
/de*l*:la   plat∫ida   mari:na   *le*   freska<u>u</u>re_a   respi<u>r</u>ar/

(...to breathe the fresh breezes of the placid seaside.)

15. /ʎ/, TURNED Y   *Voiced palatal lateral approximant*

Articulation: Tongue blade against the upper incisors and alveolar ridge.
Teeth: Separated.
Tongue tip: Touching the lower incisors (or pointing toward them).
Tongue blade: Touching the upper incisors and the forward part of the palate.
Tongue body: Narrow, avoiding contact with the teeth at the sides.
Air flow: Through the mouth, on both sides of the tongue.

Comparison

English does not have this sound, but some forms of Spanish do.

When the consonant is finished, the tongue either goes to the /i/ position or goes through the /i/ position on the way to some other vowel. Because our ears are attuned to English sounds, we interpret this movement as the semivowel /j/. Italians do not hear it that way and do not use /j/ to transcribe it.

There is a slight, but distinct difference between /lj/ and /ʎ/, specifically in the tongue position. This is how to discover the Italian sound /ʎ/:

- Say the English words "bell ye" /bɛl ji/, and notice that the apex of the tongue strikes the alveolar ridge.

- Now say the words again, with the apex of the tongue touching the lower teeth. The result will be the Italian word *begli* /bɛ<u>ʎ</u>:ʎi/ (beautiful, masc. plural).

The difference between /lj/ and /ʎ/ is so slight that even Italians sometimes exchange one for the other. The difference shows up in a common household phrase, *aglio e olio* /a<u>ʎ</u>:ʎo e <u>ɔ</u>ljo/ (garlic and oil).

Track 29

GLI is pronounced /ʎi/ if there is no other vowel in the syllable. If GLI is followed by another vowel or by /w/, the I is not pronounced, even if the vowel or /w/ is in a separate word.

Gemination

GLI /ʎ:ʎ/ is a sung double, and it is always geminated between two vowels (even in different words). The tongue rises to make the palatal contact at the end of the first syllable. Vocal tone continues until the tongue lowers again for the next vowel. If the two syllables are on different pitches, the consonant is sung on both.

Spelling: GLI.

gli scherzi	/ʎi skɛrtsi/	the jokes, pranks
degli scherzi	/deʎːʎi skɛrtsi/	of the jokes, pranks
begli occhi	/bɛʎːʎɔkːki/	beautiful eyes
la figlia	/fiʎːʎa/	daughter
il figlio, i figli	/fiʎːʎo fiʎːʎi/	son, sons
i figlioli, figliuoli	/fiʎːʎɔːli fiʎːʎwɔːli/	good sons
agli uomini	/aʎːʎwɔːmini/	to the men
gli gnomi	/ʎiɲːɲɔːmi/	the gnomes

There are no clusters with /ʎ/.

Stecchetti, Sibella: *Un organetto suona per la via,* mm. 31–35.
From *Gateway to Italian Art Songs*, page 206.

...non   so   per - ché   mi   sal - ga il   pian-to a - *gl'oc* - chi...
/non   sɔ   perke   mi   salga il   pjanto a ʎːʎɔkːki/

(...I don't know why a tear comes to my eye.)

Some uncommon words, unlikely to occur in singing, have the spelling GLI with the sounds /gl/, such as:

Anglia	/aŋglja/	Anglia
negligere	/negliːdʒere/	to neglect

𝒯𝒽𝑒 𝒯𝓇𝒾𝓁𝓁 𝒞𝑜𝓃𝓈𝑜𝓃𝒶𝓃𝓉

The letter R stands for a wide variety of different sounds in European languages. Italian R is formed by the tip of the tongue striking the alveolar ridge one or more times, in either a tap or a trill. The forms of R used in Italian are heard only in certain dialects of English.

16. /r/, LOWER-CASE R (Trill R)   *Voiced alveolar trill*

/ɾ/, FISH-HOOK R (Tap R)   *Voiced alveolar tap*

Articulation: Tongue tip and the alveolar ridge.
Lips: Relaxed before bright vowels, rounded before dark vowels. (A final R maintains the lip position of the preceding vowel.)
Tongue tip: Vibrating against the alveolar ridge.
Tongue body: Sides raised to contact the upper molars and form a narrow channel for the breath.
Air flow: Through the mouth only. The breath stream causes the tongue to tap passively against the alveolar ridge.

Tap R /ɾ/ is made with a single quick tap of the tongue tip against the alveolar ridge. Trill R /r/ is made when the tongue tip strikes two or more times against the alveolar ridge. The two sounds are allophones.

Comparison

Italian Tap R is the same as the Tap R heard in British or highly formal American English. It is simply a light, quick /d/ between vowels. Practice it in words like "very" (veddy), "sorry" (soddy), "arise" (adise).

Trill R is not needed for good English, although some singers use it in formal circumstances. (In English, Trill R carries a risk of sounding affected or foreign.) Trill R comes easily for some singers and only after long practice for others. Certain factors must be present:

> Are there Italians who cannot trill an R? Yes, even some singers. They usually substitute a French uvular R, /ʀ/, which is regarded as a speech defect, but a chic one.

- the breath stream must be energetic and must be focused through the lengthwise channel formed by the tongue;

- the apex of the tongue must be relaxed enough to tap in the breath stream;

- the apex must be precisely placed, close enough to the alveolar ridge so that the breath causes it to tap;

- the vocal folds must vibrate and produce tone;

- the singer must allow enough time for the multiple taps.

Many singers fail to trill an R because they do not allow enough time for it. A good Italian R takes a significant amount of time; in some tempos a Trill R alone will take as much time as an 8th note. If a word begins with consonants such as BR, FR or GR, the singer has to begin the consonants noticeably early so that the vowel arrives on the musical beat.

All R's must be voiced. Voiceless R exists in Spanish, but not in Italian.

Correct use of R is the most obvious single feature of good Italian diction. If an American or English R intrudes into an Italian aria, it detracts from any other good work the singer has done on diction.

Gemination

RR /rːr/ is a sung double. Vocal tone continues throughout the Trill. If the two syllables are on different pitches, the last tap of the Trill is on the second pitch.

Which, /r/ or /ɾ/?

In spoken Italian, R usually receives two or three taps but the exact number is indeterminate. One tap is also acceptable in weaker syllables.

In sung Italian, the usage may also vary, but the more careful singers and coaches follow a simple rule: *Use Tap R for a single R between two vowels and Trill R in all other situations*, namely in these cases:

1) R initial in a sentence, phrase or word;

2) R final in a sentence, phrase or word, including truncated words;

3) R before a consonant;

4) R after a consonant.

In informal speech, and therefore in comic recitatives, a Tap R may be used instead of a Trill R in less important words. On the other hand, a skilled comic actor certainly understands the effect of exaggerating a trill R, as one can hear on many recordings of Rossini operas.

Track 30

If two words are linked together by a single R, the pronunciation varies. If the first word ends in R, it is a tap.

far amore	/fa<u>ra</u>mo:re/	to make love

If the second word begins with R, it is a trill like any other initial R.

hai ragione	/a<u>i</u>:rrad<u>ʒo</u>:ne/	you are right

Spellings:

1) R, pronounced /ɾ/ between two vowels in the same word, or final before a word beginning with a vowel.

caro	/ka:ɾo/	dear
un cor amante	/un k<u>ɔ</u>:ɾam<u>a</u>nte/	a loving heart

2) R, RR, in any other situation, pronounced /r/.

la romanza	/rom<u>a</u>ndza	/song, romance
v'entrar	/ventr<u>a</u>r/	they came in here
l'arte	/<u>a</u>rte/	art
il fratello	/frat<u>ɛ</u>l:lo/	brother
il carro	/k<u>a</u>r:ro/	wagon

These words contain both Trill R and Tap R.

l'errore	/er:r<u>o</u>:ɾe/	error
l'ardore	/ard<u>o</u>:ɾe/	ardor
comprare	/kompra:ɾe/	to buy
correre	/k<u>o</u>r:reɾe/	to run

Clusters: /rj/, /rw/. See /br/, /fr/, /gr/, /kr/, /pr/, /str/, /tr/, /zr/.

l'aria	/la:ɾja/	air
la ruota	/rw<u>ɔ</u>:ta/	wheel

Stecchetti, Tosti: *Donna, vorrei morir,* mm. 2–5.
From *Gateway to Italian Art Songs*, page 179.

(Lady, I would like to die, but comforted by your sincere love.)

Stop Consonants

English and Italian have the same six stop consonants, called so because they interrupt the flow of the singer's breath. A more technical term for a stop is "plosive," which suggests that after the stop the breath "explodes" into tone again. In Italian the vowel starts gently and efficiently, without the extra expenditure of air that we call aspiration. (Aspiration may be used for dramatic effect on the operatic stage, but not in normal speech or singing.)

During a voiced stop consonant the vocal folds produce a tone that is heard inside the closed-off mouth. One can easily check the presence of the vocal fold vibration by feeling the throat or by listening to the tone with a finger stopping one ear. When the breath flow is released, a vowel is heard immediately.

17. /p/, LOWER-CASE P   *Voiceless bilabial plosive*

Articulation: Both lips.
Lips: Closed completely, without tension. Pursed if the following
vowel is rounded.
Teeth: Slightly separated.
Tongue tip: Rests behind the lower incisors.
Tongue body: Shaped for the coming vowel.
Air flow: Through the mouth only. Breath pressure builds up only slightly
before the lips open to release the vowel.

Comparison

Italian /p/ is gentler and does not have the burst of air that an emphatic /p/ has
in English. You can test this by holding a piece of paper vertically, close in
front of your mouth; it should tremble only a little, if at all, while you say this
sentence.

Track 31

Papà parte per Pisa.   /papa parte per piːza/   Dad is leaving for Pisa.

Gemination

PP /pːp/ is a stopped double. As in the English expression "top pay," the lips
close for the first P. The position is held /pː/, producing a momentary silence.
Breath flow starts again with the second P, which is released gently. The
silence between the stop and the release is essential to understanding the word.

Spelling: P, PP.

il popolo	/pɔːpolo/	people
il capello, i capelli	/kapelːlo kapelːli/	hair
il cappello	/kapːpɛlːlo/	hat
la cappella	/kapːpɛlːla/	chapel

Clusters: /pj/, /pw/, /pl/, /prj/, /pr/, /ps/. Also see /sp/.

piú	/pju/	more
può	/pwɔ/	is able
placido	/plaːtʃido/	peaceful
proprio	/prɔːprjo/	one's own
psicofisico	/psikofiːziko/	psycho-physical

A. Scarlatti: *Faria la pena mia,* mm. 108–111.
From *Gateway to Italian Art Songs,* page 38.

Fa-ria la *pe*-na mi - a *pian* - ge - re, *pian* - ge-re i sas - si
/faria la peːna miːa pjandʒere pjandʒerei sasːsi/

(My pain would make the rocks weep.)

18. /b/, LOWER-CASE B   *Voiced bilabial plosive*

Articulation
Exactly the same as /p/, with the addition of tone provided by the vocal folds. Vocal tone resonates in the mouth space behind closed lips, and there is no explosive sound when the lips open.

Comparison
Italian /b/ is gentler and less energetic than English /b/. Voicing is essential, even on high tones. Without it, /p/ is heard by mistake or no consonant is heard at all.

Just as in English, be sure that /b/ is sung on the same pitch as the following vowel. Be sure that no sound of /m/ is sung unintentionally before an initial /b/.

Gemination
BB /bːb/ is a sung double. As in the English expression "grab-bag," the lips close for the first B. Vocal tone continues until the second B opens to a vowel. If the two syllables are on different pitches, the consonant is sung on both.

No air escapes through either the mouth or the nose during /bːb/, but vocal tone continues. The sound is brief because the breath is stopped, but it must be audible.

Spelling: B, BB.

il basso	/basːso/	bass
il babbo, babbino	/babːbo babːbiːno/	daddy, dear daddy

Clusters: /bj/, /bw/, /bl/, /br/. Make sure that the /b/ is fully voiced and that there is no extra, indefinite vowel between the two initial consonants. Also see /zb/.

abbia	/abːbja/	may have
buono	/bwɔːno/	good
l'emblema	/emblɛːma/	emblem
il brodo	/brɔːdo/	broth

Conti: Dubbio di vostra fede, mm. 30–33.
From *Gateway to Italian Art Songs,* page 44.

Ti - ran-na ge - lo - si - a   non spen-se,   nò,   ma ac - cre*b-be* il mio *bel*   fɔ - co,
/tiranːna dʒeloziːa   non spɛnse   nɔ   makːkrebːbe il   mio bɛl   fɔːko/

(Tyrannical jealousy did not extinguish, no, it increased my beautiful ardor.)

19. /t/, LOWER-CASE T   *Voiceless dental plosive*

Articulation: Tongue touching all of the upper teeth.
Lips: Open.
Teeth: Slightly separated.
Tongue tip: Touching the back of the upper incisors.
Tongue body: Relaxed, with the sides raised to contact all of the upper teeth.
Air flow: Through the mouth only. Breath pressure builds up only slightly before the tongue tip drops open to release the vowel.

Comparison

English /t/ is articulated against the alveolar ridge, but Italian /t/ is formed against the teeth. A correctly dentalized /t/ is gentler and does not have the burst of air that an emphatic /t/ has in English. The absence of aspiration causes some people to think that "it sounds like D." A breathy sounding /t/ is a conspicuous sign of poor Italian.

Gemination

TT /tːt/ is a stopped double. As in the English expression "that time," the lips close for the first T. The /t/ position is held, producing a momentary silence. Breath flow starts again with the second T, which is released as described above. The silence between the stop and the release is essential to understanding the word.

Spellings: T, TT.

il tono	/tɔːno/	tone, shade	Track 33
fatale	/fataːle/	inevitable, fatal	
l'aspetto	/aspɛtːto/	appearance	

Clusters: /tj/, /tw/, /tr/. Also see /st/, /str/.

tiene	/tjɛːne/	holds
il tuono	/twɔːno/	lightning
il trillo	/trilːlo/	trill

Note: The cluster /ts/ is spelled with Z and is described as an affricate on page 70.

Puccini: *Sole e amore*, mm. 3–4.
From *Gateway to Italian Art Songs*, page 198.

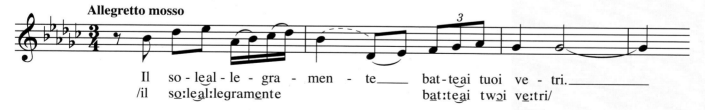

(The sun happily knocks at your windows.)

20. /d/, LOWER-CASE D

Voiced dental plosive

Articulation
Exactly the same as /t/, with the addition of tone provided by the vocal folds. Vocal tone is resonated behind in the mouth space behind the tongue, and there is no explosive sound as the vowel starts.

Comparison
For English /d/ the tongue strikes against the alveolar ridge, but for Italian /d/ the tongue strikes the upper incisors. Voicing is essential, even on high tones. Without it, /t/ is heard by mistake.

Just as in English, be sure that /d/ is sung on the same pitch as the following vowel. Be sure that no sound of /n/ is sung unintentionally before an initial /d/.

Gemination
DD /dːd/ is a sounded double. As in the English expression "sad day," the tongue closes for the first D. Vocal tone continues as the D position is held. An impulse of breath energy begins the second D, which opens as described above.

No air escapes through either the mouth or the nose during /dːd/, but vocal tone continues. The sound is brief because the breath is stopped, but it must be audible.

Track 34

Spellings: D, DD.

la donna	/dɔnːna/	woman
la spada	/spaːda/	sword
addio	/adːdio/	farewell

Clusters: /dj/, /dw/, /dr/. Also see /zd/.

il podio	/pɔːdjo/	platform
il duomo	/dwɔːmo/	cathedral
il dramma	/dramːma/	drama

The cluster /dz/ is spelled with Z and is described as an affricate on page 71.

The cluster /dʒ/ is spelled with G and is described as an affricate on pages 73–74.

Heine, Ponchielli: *Dimenticar, ben mio,* mm. 22–25.
From *Gateway to Italian Art Songs*, page 173.

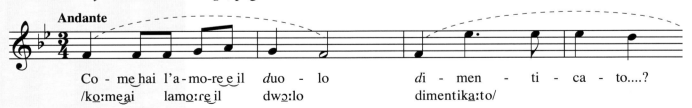

(How have you forgotten the love and the sorrow...?)

21. /k/, LOWER-CASE K   *Voiceless velar plosive*

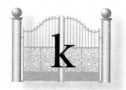

Articulation: Tongue body against the hard palate and upper molars.
Lips: Open, shaped for the following vowel.
Teeth: Separated.
Tongue tip: Touching the lower incisors.
Tongue body: Raised, contacting the hard palate and upper molars.
Air flow: Through the mouth only. Breath pressure builds up only slightly before the tongue drops to release the vowel.

Comparison

Italian /k/ is gentler and does not have the burst of air (aspiration) that an emphatic /k/ has in English. The absence of aspiration causes some people to think that "it sounds like G." A breathy sounding /k/ is a conspicuous sign of poor Italian.

The exact point of articulation varies, being farther forward after bright vowels. It is beneficial for singing to form /k/ as far forward on the palate as possible.

Gemination

KK /k:k/ is a stopped double. As in the English expression "black cow," the tongue closes off the breath for the first /k/. The /k/ position is held, producing a momentary silence. Breath flow starts again with the second /k/. The silence between the stop and the release is essential to understanding the word.

If QU /kw/ is geminated, it is spelled CQU, not QQU. As in the English expression "talk quickly," the silence between the stop and the release is essential to understanding the word.

Spellings:

 Track 35

1) C or CC before A, O, U or a consonant (H, R, or L).

il canto	/kanto/	singing
la coda	/koːda/	tail
Bacco	/bakːko/	Bacchus
il tacchino	/takːkiːno/	turkey

2) CH or CCH before E or I.

l'orchestra	/orkɛstra/	orchestra
le bocche	/bokːke/	mouths

3) QU, CQU.

quanto	/kwanto/	how much
l'aquila	/aːkwila/	eagle
tacqui	/takːkwi/	I was silent

4) X in the cluster /ks/.

lo xilofono	/ksilɔːfono/	xylophone

Clusters: /kj/, /kw/, /kl/, /kr/, /ks/ (above). Also see /sk/, /skr/.

la chiesa	/kjɛːza/	church
il cuoio	/kwɔːjo/	leather
classico	/klasːsiko/	classical
occludere	/okːkluːdeɾe/	to block
crudo, -a	/kruːdo/	harsh, raw

A. Scarlatti: *Alfin m'ucciderete,* mm. 22–24.
From *Gateway to Italian Art Songs,* page 26.

E *chi* sa *che* *que*-st'o - ra,   già scor-da - ta di me,   non l'a-mi an-co-ra?
/e ki sa ke kwestoːra   dʒa skordaːta di me   non laːmi aŋkoːra/

(And who knows whether, already having forgotten me, she is not already in love with him?)

Note: For the spellings CE and CI, see the affricate /tʃ/ on page 72.

22. /g/, LOWER-CASE G   *Voiced velar plosive*

Articulation
Exactly the same as /k/, with the addition of tone provided by the vocal folds. Vocal tone is resonated in the mouth and pharynx behind the tongue, and there is no explosive sound as the vowel starts.

Comparison
English and Italian /g/ are exactly the same. Voicing is essential, even on high tones. Without it, /k/ is heard by mistake.

Just as in the case of /k/, it is beneficial for a singer to articulate /g/ farther forward in singing than in speech. As in English, be sure that /g/ is sung on the same pitch as the following vowel.

Gemination
GG /gːg/ is a sung double. As in the English expression "big game," the tongue forms the first G. Vocal tone continues until the second G opens to a vowel. If the two syllables are on different pitches, the consonant is sung on both.

No air escapes through either the mouth or the nose during /gːg/, but vocal tone continues. The sound is brief because the breath is stopped, but it must be audible.

 Track 36   **Spellings:**
1) G or GG before A, O, U or a consonant (H, R, or L).

la gavotta	/gavɔtːta/	gavotte (a Baroque dance)
largo	/laɾgo/	broad
struggo	/strugːgo/	I-suffer

2) GH or GGH before E or I.

il ghetto	/ˈget:to/	ghetto
gli spaghetti	/spaˈget:ti/	spaghetti

Clusters: /gj/, /gw/, /gl/, /gr/. Also see /zg/.

agghiaccia	/ag:ˈgjat:tʃa/	chills
la guancia	/ˈgwantʃa/	cheek
glissando	/glisˈsando/	gliding
grande	/ˈgrande/	large

M. Maggioni, Marietta Brambilla: *L'Allegro,* mm. 25–29.

...del pre - sen - te vo' go - der,   del pre - sen - te vo' go - der.
/del   prezɛnte   vɔ goder/

(... I want to enjoy the present.)

Note: For the spellings GE and GI, see the affricate /dʒ/ on page 73. For GL see /ʎ/ on page 55. For GN see /ɲ/ on page 52.

Fricative Consonants

Fricative consonants partially interfere with the breath flow, so that there is a sound of air turbulence. Because they do not stop the breath, they can be prolonged. The fricative consonants that have a hissing sound, such as /s, z, ʃ/, may also be called SIBILANTS.

23. /f/, LOWER-CASE F   *Voiceless labiodental fricative*

Articulation: Lower lip against the upper teeth.
Lips: Closed at the sides, open at the center, lower lip lightly touching the edges of the upper incisors.
Teeth: Separated.
Tongue tip: Touching the lower incisors.
Air flow: Only through the narrow opening between the lower lip and the upper teeth with enough pressure to make air turbulence.

Comparison
Italian and English /f/ are exactly the same. The PH spelling never occurs.

Gemination
FF /f:f/ is a sounded double. As in the phrase "half fried," the breath stream and its frictional noise continue between the syllabic vowels. If desired for expressive reasons, the second F can be emphasized with a breath impulse.

Spellings: F, FF.

Track 37

la festa	/ˈfɛsta/	party, celebration
il caffè	/kafˈfɛ/	coffee

Clusters: /fj/, /fw/, /fl/, /fr/. Also see /sf/.

il fiato	/fjaːto/	breath
il fuoco	/fwɔːko/	fire
il flauto	/flauto/	flute
il fratello	/fratɛlːlo/	brother

Pepoli, Rossini: *La Pastorella,* mm. 22–25.
From *Gateway to Italian Art Songs*, page 101.

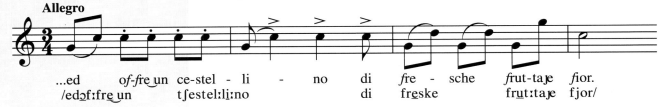

...ed   *of-fre̠* un ce-stel - li - no   di *fre* - sche   *frut-ta̠je fjor.*
/edɔfːfre̠ un tʃestelːliːno   di freske   frutːta̠je fjor/

(... and offers a little basket of fresh fruits and flowers.)

24. /v/, LOWER-CASE V   *Voiced labiodental fricative*

Articulation
Exactly the same as /f/, with the addition of tone provided by the vocal folds. The sound of /v/ is the sound of vocal tone emerging with air turbulence through a narrow slit between the lower lip and the upper teeth.

Comparison
Italian /v/ sounds exactly the same as English /v/.

As a voiced consonant, /v/ fits smoothly into a legato line. You can use it like a hum to vocalize throughout your range.

Gemination
VV /vːv/ is a sung double. As in the phrase "love violets," the breath stream and its voiced frictional sound continue between the syllabic vowels. If desired for expressive reasons, the second V can be emphasized with a breath impulse.

Track 38

Spelling:
1) V, VV.

la voce	/voːtʃe/	voice
avvezzo	/avːveːtːtso/	accustomed

2) W, in foreign names

Le Willi	/vilːli/	Puccini's first opera

Cluster: /vj/, /vw/, /vr/. See also: /zv/.

il viaggio	/vjaḏːdʒo/	journey
vuoto	/vwɔːto/	empty
sovrano	/sovraːno/	sovereign

Conti: *Dopo tante e tante pene,* mm. 3–4.
From *Gateway to Italian Art Songs*, page 44.

pu - re̠al-fin   a *v*oi   ri-tor - no, *v*a - ghe   lu - ci__   del   mio   ben.
/puːre̠alfin   a *v*oi   ritorno   vaːge   luːtʃi   del   mio   bɛn/

(... then at last to you I return, lovely eyes of my beloved.)

25. /s/, LOWER-CASE S   *Voiceless alveolar fricative*

Articulation: Between tongue tip (or blade) and alveolar ridge.

Lips: Open, shaped for the following vowel.

Teeth: Separated.

Tongue tip: Near the alveolar ridge (or pointed toward the lower incisors).

Tongue body: Sides raised to contact the upper molars and form a narrow channel for the breath.

Air flow: Only through the small horizontal slit formed between the tongue tip (or blade) and the alveolar ridge, issuing with a hissing sound.

Comparison

Italian /s/ sounds exactly the same as English /s/. The hissing noise of /s/ does not have a specific pitch, but its pitch range is much higher than that of /ʃ/.

Pronounce /s/ quickly; it is usually easy to hear, even when sung by singers who have poor diction otherwise. Prolong /s/ slightly if it is doubled.

Gemination

SS /sːs/ is a sounded double. As in the phrase "this song," the breath stream and its hissing noise continue. If desired for expressive reasons, the second S can be emphasized with a breath impulse.

Spellings: S (except between two vowels or before a voiced consonant), SS.   Track 39

sono	/soːno/	I am
intenso	/intɛnso/	intense
posso	/pɔsːso/	I can

Caution: Initial S keeps its normal pronunciation (and does not change to /z/) after a prefix or between two joined words.

risorto (ri-sorto)	/risorto/	risen again
trentasei	/trentasɛi/	thirty-six
stasera (questa sera)	/staseːra/	this evening

Clusters: /sj/, /sw/, /sf/, /sk/, /skr/, /sp/, /spl/, /spr/, /st/, /str/.
Also see /ps/, /ks/.

la passione	/pasːsjoːne/	passion
il suono	/swɔːno/	sound
la sfera	/sfɛːra/	sphere
lo scherzo	/skertso/	joke, prank
iscritto	/iskritːto/	in writing
respiro	/respiːro/	I breathe
risplendere	/risplɛndere/	to sparkle
lo spregio	/sprɛːdʒo/	contempt
resta	/rɛsta/	remains
la strada	/straːda/	street

Vincenzo Bellini: *Il Zeffiro*, mm. 6–10.
From *Gateway to Italian Art Songs*, page 136.

(... you go fluttering around me, [tell me] if you saw my beloved.)

26. /z/, LOWER-CASE Z   *Voiced alveolar fricative*

Articulation
Exactly the same as /s/, with the addition of tone provided by the vocal folds. The sound of /z/ is the sound of vocal tone emerging through a narrow slit between the front edge of the tongue (or the blade) and the alveolar ridge.

Comparison
Italian /z/ sounds exactly the same as English /z/. The difference is in spelling: In Italian this sound is spelled only with S, never with Z.

Intervocalic S is pronounced /z/ in modern standard Italian. Singers prefer this pronunciation because it does not interrupt the vocal fold vibration. In Tuscan dialect intervocalic S is pronounced /z/ in some words and /s/ in others; for instance, *casa* is pronounced /kaːsa/ in Tuscan, as it is in Spanish. Some dictionaries still show a preference for the Tuscan pronunciation, but singers should ignore it.

In English, if /z/ and another consonant occur together, as in "jasmine," they always belong to different syllables. In Italian, /z/ and another consonant may be combined in a cluster at the beginning of a syllable or word. Voicing /z/ before a voiced consonant is essential and requires practice.

Gemination
SS is always voiceless and therefore /z/ is never geminated in Italian.

Spellings: S between two vowels, except for compounds (see under /s/).

la casa	/kaːza/	house
cosí	/kozi/	thus, that's how
l'inglese	/li˜gleːze/	Englishman

Track 40

Clusters: S before any voiced consonant is pronounced /z/, resulting in these possible combinations: /zj/, /zb/, /zd/, /zgw/, /zdʒ/, /zl/, /zm/, /zn/, /zr/ and /zv/.

l'Asia	/aːzja/	Asia
lo sbaglio	/zbaʎːʎo/	mistake
lo sdegno	/zdeꞁːꞁo/	disdain
lo sguardo	/zgwardo/	gaze, glance
lo sgelo	/zdʒɛːlo/	thaw, melting
sleale	/zleaːle/	disloyal
la smania	/zmaːnja/	restlessness
snello	/znɛlːlo/	slim
israelitico	/izraeliːtiko/	Jewish
la sventura	/zventuːra/	misfortune

Donizetti: *Che vuoi di più?*, mm. 6–10.
From *Gateway to Italian Art Songs*, page 117.

Un	so-spir	tuo	non	ren - de sgom	- bro	di	nu - bi	il____	ciel?
/un	sospir	tuo	non	rɛnde zgombro		di	nuːbi	il	tʃɛl/

(Doesn't a sigh of yours render the sky cleared of clouds?)

27. /ʃ/, Esh

Voiceless postalveolar fricative

Articulation: Between tongue blade and alveolar ridge.
Lips: Moderately rounded and projected forward.
Teeth: Separated more than for /s/.
Tongue tip: Pointing downward.
Tongue blade: Near the alveolar ridge.
Tongue body: Sides raised to contact the upper molars, forming a wider breath channel than for /s/.
Air flow: Only through the small horizontal slit formed between the tongue blade and the alveolar ridge, issuing with a hissing sound. The pitch of the sibilant noise is indefinite, but lower than that of /s/.

Comparison

Italian /ʃ/ resembles the English SH except for lip rounding, which lowers the pitch. English /ʃ/ has rounded lips before rounded vowels, as in "shoe," but not before bright vowels, as in "she." Unrounded /ʃ/ has a comparatively harsh sound.

Notice that in the spellings SCIA, SCIO and SCIU the I is not pronounced. It is present only to indicate a "soft" pronunciation.

The voiced counterpart of /ʃ/ is /ʒ/, which is the medial consonant in "pleasure." /ʒ/ occurs in Italian dialects, but not in the standard language.

Gemination

Intervocalic SC or SCI /ʃːʃ/ is a sounded double; it is always geminated, never single, even between two words.

Spellings:

1) SC before E or I.

la scena	/laʃːʃɛːna/	scene
la scimmia	/laʃːʃimːmja/	monkey
crescendo	/kreʃːʃɛndo/	growing

2) SCI before A, O or U.

lasciate	/laʃːʃate/	you (pl.) let
sciolto	/ʃɔlto/	untied
asciutto	/aʃːʃutːto/	dry

Because of their derivation from Latin a few words have SCI before E, with the I remaining silent.

la coscienza	/koʃːʃɛntsa/	conscience

There are no clusters with /ʃ/.

Rossini: *Chi m'ascolta il canto usato,* mm. 11–18.
From *Gateway to Italian Art Songs,* page 88.

(Whoever hears my customary song ringing out happily sometimes...)

Affricates

An affricate is a combination of a stop plosive and a sibilant consonant produced at the same location. The IPA uses two symbols together for an affricate, but the listener hears the combination as a single sound.

For affricates, Canepàri uses the term *semiocclusivo* to indicate that the first half of each sound is occluded (closed). He uses merged symbols, such as /dz/, which symbolize the fact that an affricate is heard as a single sound, although merged forms are no longer used by the International Phonetic Association. For a geminated affricate, Canepàri doubles the symbol, for instance, /tʃtʃ/, but only the stop should be geminated (as in "coat check"), not the complete affricate (as in "each check").

28. /ts/, T-S AFFRICATE   *Voiceless dental affricate*

Articulation
The breath is stopped by a dentalized /t/ and released, as the tongue moves through an /s/ position on its way to the following vowel.

Comparison
Italian /ts/ resembles the medial consonant in the name Mozart /mo̱tsart/, spoken with a dental /t/. It occurs only within a word; for words that begin with Z, see the voiced affricate /dz/.

Gemination
Intervocalic Z or ZZ /tːts/ is a stopped double. We might use it in English when we ask, "Is that so?" with a skeptical inflection. Intervocalic Z is always geminated, within a word or between two words and even if there is only one Z in the spelling.

Track 42   **Spellings:** Z, ZZ, in medial position in some words.

marzo	/ma̱ːrtso/	March
Enzo	/ɛ̱ntso/	male name
la pizza	/pi̱ːtsa/	pizza
la grandezza	/grande̱ːtsa/	size

Clusters: /tːtsj/, /tːtsw/.

grazie	/gra̱ːtsje/	thanks
il mazzuolo	/matːtswɔ̱ːlo/	mallet

The musical example follows unit 29, the D-Z affricate.

Notice: Z and ZZ within a word are sometimes voiceless /ts/ and sometimes voiced /dz/. There are no adequate rules to follow. Rely on a good dictionary.

29. /dz/, D-Z AFFRICATE   *Voiced dental affricate*

Articulation
Exactly like /ts/, with the addition of vocal tone.

Comparison
Italian /dz/ resembles the final sound in English "gods," except that the /d/ is dentalized.

In Tuscan dialect, and therefore in older dictionaries, initial Z is voiced in some words and voiceless in others. The simpler, more modern practice is to voice initial Z in all words. Within a word, Z is sometimes voiced, sometimes voiceless, differing from word to word. There are no adequate rules to distinguish one from the other. Rely on a good dictionary.

Gemination
Z or ZZ /dːdz/ is a sung double. We hear a similar sound in "good zone." Medial Z is always geminated, even between two words and even if there is only one Z in the spelling.

Be sure that your vocal tone is continuous through the prolonged consonant.

Spellings: Z, ZZ, in initial position and in some words.   *Track 43*

bronzo	/brondzo/	bronze
la romanza	/romandza/	romance, song
lo zeffiretto	/lodːdzefːfirːetːto/	little breeze
la mezzosoprano	/mɛdːdzosopraːno/	mezzo-soprano singer
la gazza	/gadːdza/	magpie

Cluster: /dːdzj/.

l'azienda	/adːdzjɛnda/	business firm

Notice: Z and ZZ are also the spellings of the previous phoneme.

Donizetti: *Se a te d'intorno scherza,* mm. 3–7.
From *Gateway to Italian Art Songs,* page 121.

(If around you plays a new little breeze,....)

30. /tʃ/, T-Esh AFFRICATE *Voiceless postalveolar affricate*

Articulation
The breath is stopped, either at the upper incisors or in the postalveolar area, and released in an /ʃ/. The lips are rounded and protruded.

Comparison
Italian /tʃ/ resembles the initial sound in English "chew," but there are significant differences. Some English speakers produce the sound rather far back on the palate; a more forward tongue placement is advantageous for singing.

After /l/ or /n/, which are dentalized in Italian, this affricate begins from the position of a dental /t/. Otherwise, the closure is postalveolar and is made by the blade of the tongue, with the tip pointing downward.

In English, the lips are not involved. Italian lip rounding lowers the pitch range of the consonant, making the sound less harsh.

Canepàri describes /tʃ/ as *"postalveo-palato-labiale"* because of the postalveolar closure, lifting of the tongue toward the palate for /ʃ/, and the protrusion of the lips. All of these things must occur.

Gemination
CC /tːtʃ/ is a stopped double. The sound is like that in English "that child," not like the double articulation in "which child." Italian pronouncing dictionaries may show the symbols /tʃtʃ/ for CC, but there is only one closure and one release.

The silence made by holding the stop is essential to understanding the word.

Spellings:

1) C or CC before E or I

vivace	/vivaːtʃe/	lively
facile	/faːtʃile/	easy
il violoncello	/violontʃɛlːlo/	cello
le facce	/fatːtʃe/	faces
i lacci	/latːtʃi/	bonds, ties
Puccini	/putːtʃiːni/	composer

2) CI or CCI before A, O or U (Notice that the letter I is silent.)

Francia	/frantʃa/	France
cioccolato	/tʃokːkolaːto/	chocolate
la facciata	/fatːtʃaːta/	facade
il laccio	/latːtʃo/	bond, tie
il ciuccio	/tʃutːtʃo/	baby's pacifier

Notice: The letter I is usually silent in the letter groups CIA, CIO and CIU. A few words spelled with CIA have the letter I pronounced and stressed, but they are not frequent in singing. One name, Lucia, is an important exception.

Lucia	/lutʃiːa/	operatic role
la farmacia	/farmatʃiːa/	pharmacy

A few words, because of their Latin derivation, have a spelling CIE in which the superfluous I is silent.

il cielo	/tʃɛːlo/	heaven
cieco, -a	/tʃɛːko tʃɛːka/	blind
l'arciere	/artʃɛːre/	archer

There are no clusters with /tʃ/.

Aldighieri, Arditi: *Il Bacio,* mm. 32–38.
From *Gateway to Italian Art Songs*, page 161.

dol-*ce* un ba - *cio*   ti   da - re - i,   dol-*ce* un ba - *cio*   ti___   da - rei.
/d<u>o</u>lt<u>ʃe</u> un ba<u>ː</u>tʃo   ti   dar<u>ɛ</u>ːi/

(... I would give you a sweet kiss.)

31. /dʒ/, D-Yogh AFFRICATE   *Voiced affricate*

Articulation
Exactly like /tʃ/, with the addition of vocal tone.

Comparison
English and Italian /dʒ/ sound the same. Some English speakers may produce the sound rather far back on the palate; the more forward tongue placement described for /tʃ/ is advantageous for singing.

In English, the lips are not involved. Italian speech authorities insist that the lips must be slightly "advanced" for this sound in standard Italian, even though the difference in sound is only slight.

Voicing is essential even on high tones. Without it, /tʃ/ is heard by mistake.

Gemination
GG /dːdʒ/ is a sung double. The sound is like that in English "red gem," not like the double articulation in "large gem." Italian pronouncing dictionaries may show the symbols /dʒdʒ/ for GG, but there is only one closure and one release.

Vocal tone continues while the /d/ position is held. If the two syllables are on different pitches, /d/ is sung on the first and /dʒ/ on the second.

Spellings:
1) G or GG before E or I

Track 45

gelo	/dʒ<u>ɛ</u>ːlo/	I freeze
la laringe	/lar<u>i</u>ndʒe/	larynx
la giga	/dʒiːga/	jig
struggere	/str<u>u</u>dːdʒere/	to-melt
raggi	/r<u>a</u>dːdʒi/	rays, eyes

2) GI or GGI before A, O or U

Giacomo	/dʒaːkomo/	Jacob (James)
Giovanni	/dʒovanːni/	John
Giuseppe	/dʒuzɛpːpe/	Joseph
laggiù	/ladːdʒu/	down-there

Notice: The letter I is usually silent in the letter groups GIA, GIO and GIU. There are a few words that have a stressed I in the spelling GIA and do occur in singing.

la bugia	/budʒiːa/	lie, falsehood
la magia	/madʒiːa/	magic
il leggio	/ledːdʒiːo/	music stand

A few words have an alternative spelling GIE in which the superfluous I is silent.

leggero, leggiero	/ledːdʒɛːro/	light
Ruggero, Ruggiero	/rudːdʒɛːro/	male name

There are no clusters with initial /dʒ/: See /zdʒ/.

Donizetti: *Amiamo,* mm. 72 –75.
From Donizetti *20 Songs*, Alfred Publishing Co., Inc., page 11.

(... a day without love is a day of sadness.)

Chapter 6: Diphthongs Within Words

It often happens that a single Italian syllable contains two or three vowel letters. They often form a diphthong, "a complex speech sound that begins with one vowel and changes to another vowel within the same syllable," as we said in Chapter 1.

Often in Italian a final vowel merges with the initial vowel of the next word to form a new phonosyllable; those cases are explained in Chapter 7. This chapter deals with diphthongs that occur within single words.

How Does a Diphthong Sound?

Italian scholars explain diphthongs in various ways, but in our analysis all diphthongs consist of a longer vowel and a shorter one. In singing a diphthong on a melodic note, the first element takes up nearly the full duration of the note, and the second is sung quickly at the end of the note. We will call them, respectively, the MAIN VOWEL[1] of the diphthong and the OFF-GLIDE.[2]

Italian diphthongs differ from English ones in the clarity of the off-glide. If I is the short vowel, it will always be a fully formed /i/, never /ɪ/, as it usually is in English. If U is the short vowel, it will always be a clear /u/, never /ʊ/.

Another difference is that in English the off-glide of a diphthong is always one of three vowels: /ɪ ʊ ə/. In Italian the off-glide may be any one of five: /a e i o u/. Some diphthongs occur commonly, while others are rare.

A diphthong in a stressed syllable is naturally long due to the combination of two vowels. It is not necessary to use the lengthening symbol /ː/ for a stressed diphthong.

Spelling

In spelling English diphthongs, the letters often have little to do with the pronunciation; for instance, the diphthong in "how" is spelled OW but pronounced /aʊ/. Even a single letter can stand for a diphthong; for instance, "I" is a single letter in writing, but a diphthong /aɪ/ in sound. In Italian the spelling and pronunciation match perfectly.

Identifying Diphthongs

Our definition of a diphthong seems simple and understandable but some questions arise when we consider real cases.

As always, we are dealing with sounds, not letters, so the silent I in the digraphs CI, GI and SCI does not concern us here. There are no diphthongs in words like *ciò*, *già* or *lascio* because the I is silent in such cases.

Also, the semivowels /j/ and /w/ do not form a diphthong with the vowel that follows. In words like "you" /ju/ and "we" /wi/ the semivowels function just like consonants.

A sequence of two or three vowel letters may or may not include a diphthong. In order to identify diphthongs, it is helpful to speak of two classes of vowels:

Strong vowels:	Weak vowels (or semivowels):
A /a/	I /i j/
E /e ɛ/	U /u w/
O /o ɔ/	

Any combination of two vowels will typically fit one of the following patterns.

 Track 46

1) Weak-weak (W+W), usually treated as semivowel + vowel.

| il liuto | /ljuːto/ | lute |
| la guida | /gwiːda/ | guidebook, manual |

---

[1]Some texts use other expressions, such as "syllabic vowel" or "nuclear vowel."
[2]Some texts use "vanish" vowel.

2) Weak-strong (W+S), usually treated as semivowel + vowel.

piano	/pjaːno/	slowly
la guerra	/gwɛrːra/	war
il guaio	/gwaːjo/	woe

3) Strong-strong (S+S), treated either as a diphthong or as two separate syllables.

l'aere	/aere/	atmosphere (poetic)
neonato	/neonaːto/	newborn
Paolo	/paolo/	Paul
l'idea	/idɛa/	idea
la poesia	/poezia/	poetry

4) Strong-weak (S-W), treated as diphthongs.

mai	/mai/	never
l'aura	/aura/	light breeze
lei	/lɛi/	she
Europa	/eurɔːpa/	Europe
poi	/pɔi/	then

In the first two cases, W+W and W+S, the semivowel is sung quickly and the vowel fills up the note value. (Cases in which the first, weak vowel is stressed are discussed later.) In the latter two cases the first vowel fills up nearly all the length of the note and the second vowel is sung quickly at the end.

The cases given so far are typical, but they are not the whole story. It is necessary to examine all four patterns again for other possibilities.

1) Weak-weak (W+W). There are also a few words spelled with UI in which U is the main vowel of a diphthong, as discussed later in this chapter. Italian does not have words with the sounds of English "ye" /ji/ and "woo" /wu/. Also, UU does not exist, but II does. Although the first I is stressed, the second must also be pronounced, if time allows, with a slight breath impulse.

capii	/kapii/	I understood

If the second vowel is part of a suffix, the two vowels are considered to be in separate syllables, as shown in IPA (optionally) with a period.

il taccuino	/takːku.iːno/	notebook

2) Weak-strong (W+S). There are many words in which I or U is the main vowel of a diphthong, as discussed later in this chapter. Also, if the first vowel is part of a prefix or the second vowel is part of a suffix, the two vowels may be pronounced in separate syllables, as shown in IPA with a period (dictionaries may disagree with each other on this point).

il dialogo	/di.aːlogo/	dialogue
il duetto	/du.etːto/	duet
diminuendo	/diminu.ɛndo/	getting softer

3) Strong-strong (S+S). In music, composers treat S+S combinations inconsistently. Most often, the second vowel is unstressed; musical settings of the words given as examples may use only one note for the diphthong. Or the composer may imagine the vowels as separate syllables and use a note for each one. Puccini, for instance, in setting the word *"poesia"* in *La Bohème* used separate notes for the O and E. (Mimí's Act I aria is the first instance.)

If the second vowel is stressed, it forms a separate syllable and there is no diphthong. In that case, the music will usually have a note for each syllable. The following words have three syllables, not two; the consecutive vowels are considered to be separate syllables, as shown by periods in IPA.

il poeta	/po.ɛːta/	poet
beato	/be.aːto/	blessed
soave	/so.aːve/	gentle, soft, sweet
maestro	/ma.ɛːstro/	teacher

(Again, there are exceptions, depending on the way the composer perceived the word. One can find many cases in which the two syllables are combined into a dipththong.)

4) Strong-weak (S-W). This pattern nearly always produces a diphthong, but in a few exceptional words the weak vowel is stressed. When this is the case, the music will have a note for each syllable. In the following words the consecutive vowels are not diphthongs but separate syllables, as shown by periods in IPA.

l'aita, aïta	/a.iːta/	help (poetic)
la paura	/pa.uːra/	fear
Aida, Aïda	/a.iːda/	operatic role
l'oboista	/obo.ista/	oboeist

Three or Four Consecutive Vowels

If a word contains three or four consecutive vowel letters, one or more of them will be either a silent I, a semivowel or an off-glide. Many patterns are possible, as shown by the following examples (not a complete list).

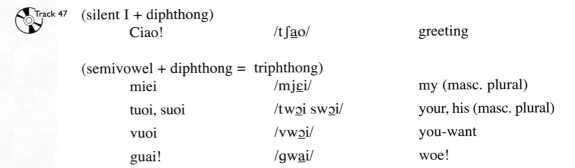

Track 47

(silent I + diphthong)

Ciao!	/tʃao/	greeting

(semivowel + diphthong = triphthong)

miei	/mjɛi/	my (masc. plural)
tuoi, suoi	/twɔi swɔi/	your, his (masc. plural)
vuoi	/vwɔi/	you-want
guai!	/gwai/	woe!

(two semivowels + vowel = triphthong)

la quiete	/kwjɛːte/	quietness
seguiamo	/segwjaːmo/	let's-follow

But the following patterns produce separate syllables (as shown by periods in IPA), not diphthongs:

(vowel + semivowel + vowel = separate syllables)

il paio	/pa̱.jo/	pair
l'aiuto	/a. juːto/	help
gaiamente	/ga.ja.me̱n.te/	cheerfully

(diphthong + semivowel + vowel = separate syllables)

| le aiuole | /ai.wɔ̱ːle/ | flower gardens |

(This is the shortest possible word that uses all five vowel letters.)

(semivowel + vowel + semivowel + vowel = separate syllables)

| il cuoiame | /kwɔ.jaːme/ | leather goods |

Again, composers treat these combinations in various ways. Earlier composers tended more to divide vowel combinations into separate syllables because they were more conscious of the derivation of words from Latin, which has no diphthongs. Since about 1800, composers have more often followed speech patterns in which vowels are combined into diphthongs.

I and U as Main Vowels

There are a number of words in which I and U are main vowels, preceding either strong or weak vowels. It is impossible to give a complete list, but the following list shows words that demonstrate typical patterns and are commonly used in lyric texts.

a) pronouns:

Track 48

io	/i̱o/	I
mio, mia, mie	/mi̱o mi̱a mi̱e/	my
tuo, tua, tue	/tu̱o, tu̱a, tu̱e/	your
suo, sua, sue	/su̱o, su̱a, su̱e/	his, hers or its
cui	/ku̱i/	whose
lui	/lu̱i/	he, him
colui, costui	/kolu̱i kostu̱i/	that man
altrui	/altru̱i/	other people's

b) in a few other words, often used in singing, that resemble *mio*:

addio	/adːdi̱o/	goodbye
il brio	/bri̱o/	brilliance
il desio	/dezi̱o/	desire
il dio, Dio, Iddio	/di̱o idːdi̱o/	god, God
l'oblio	/obli̱o/	forgetting, oblivion
natio	/nati̱o/	native (land, soil, etc.)
il trio	/tri̱o/	trio
lo zio, la zia	/dzi̱o dzi̱a/	uncle, aunt
pio, pia	/pi̱o pi̱a/	pious
rio, ria	/ri̱o ri̱a/	cruel (not "river")

c) in a relatively few words that end in *-ia*, with the plural *-ie*:

l'armonia	/armonia/	harmony
la bugia, le bugie	/budʒia budʒie/	falsehood, falsehoods
la compagnia	/kompāːˉia/	company
la fantasia	/fantazia/	fantasy
la follia	/folːlia/	folly
la magia	/madʒiːa/	magic
la melodia	/melodia/	melody, art song
pria (from *prima*)	/pria/	first, before
la sinfonia	/sinfonia/	symphony
la trattoria	/tratːtoria/	restaurant
la via	/via/	road

d) in some words with the Greek prefixes *di-, tri-*:

| la diade, la triade | /diade triade/ | dyad, triad (music theory) |

e) in some subjunctive verbs (commands or wish expressions), such as:

sia, siano	/sia siano/	may it be! may they be!
dia, diano	/dia diano/	may it/they give!
fia, fiano	/fia fiano/	may it/they be done!

With the exceptions named above, a word that ends with -IA, -IE or -IO usually has the /j/ sound. Still, proper names that end in -IA are a problem to the foreigner. To give a familiar example, there is no obvious reason why the masculine names *Mario* and *Lucio* are stressed on the first syllable and the feminine names *Maria* and *Lucia* are stressed on the second. One must learn such proper names from other persons who are familiar with them or from dictionaries. Many names are listed in Canepàri's *Dizionario di pronuncia italiana* (Zanichelli, 1999).

Past Tense Verbs

Past tense verbs ending in -EVA, -IVA, -...VANO or -ÍVANO in modern Italian often drop the V in poetry, resulting in consecutive vowels -EA- or -IA-, with the first vowel being the main one. These syllables are usually set to single notes.

 Track 49

cadea	/kadea/	he-fell, she-fell
cadeano	/kadeano/	they-fell
tacea	/tatʃea/	was-silent
moria	/moria/	he-died, she-died

Example: In *Tosca*, Act III, the tenor sings *"Mi cadea fra le braccia"* (she fell into my arms), and Puccini set *-dea* as a single syllable on a single note.

Singing Diphthongs

In singing diphthongs we must follow the same principle as in English: The main vowel is prolonged for nearly the full value of the note. The off-glide is sung quickly at the end of the note.

If another note follows, the off-glide is sung as if it were on a grace note to the next note or, alternatively, a little longer. Notice that it is sung cleanly on its proper pitch, not on the pitch of the next note.

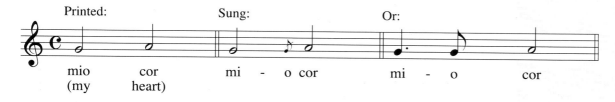

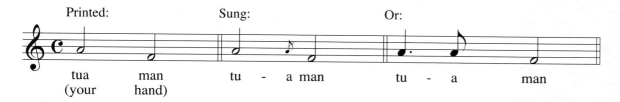

The words *mio, tuo* and *suo* are mispronounced more often than any other words by singers who do not know Italian traditions. English speakers are used to I and U as semivowels, and we are not used to singing O as a short vowel. As a result, it seems natural to sing the first vowel quickly and lengthen the second. But it is a mistake.

Also, it is not true that the note is simply divided in half between the vowels, as one may often hear from singers who do not know Italian well, but rather, the main vowel should be sung longer than the off-glide even on the shortest of notes.

When a diphthong is printed below a series of relatively long notes, the main vowel is sung on all of the notes and the short vowel is sung on the last note or at the end of the last note.

The main vowel must be sung on all of the notes that are slurred together, unless this turns out to be excessively awkward or fussy. Here is a case where the off-glide can have a note of its own, if the tempo is moderate to quick.

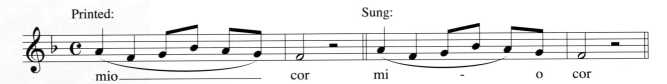

Two brief passages from a song by Vincenzo Bellini, *"Per pietà, bell' idol mio,"* (found in *Gateway to Italian Art Song*) provide an illustration of the choices that face a singer. The text is *"Il mio core, il tuo lo sa"* (My heart, and yours, knows it). Here are two phrases just as Bellini's first publisher printed them:

mm. 23–25

mm. 31–33

Notice that Bellini gave either one or two notes to the words *"mio"* and *"tuo."* The tempo is *allegro agitato*, so the diphthongs must be pronounced quickly. When words *"mio"* and *"tuo"* have two eighth-notes, they will be pronounced in two syllables, *"mi-o"* and *"tu-o."*

Modern engraving will change the appearance of this passage, but not the sound. Formerly, two eighth-notes beamed together would be sung on the same syllable, but now it is customary to add a slur also over two eighth-notes. The editor will probably hyphenate *"mi-o"* and *"tu-o."*

In this example from Rossini's *La Cenerentola* (Act I Duet), the off-glide is sung on the last note of an extended passage of quick notes.

Tempo plays an important role in the singer's decisions about diphthongs. In this example from Mozart's *Così fan tutte*, the tempo is so slow that the main vowel is sung throughout two 16th notes and still leaves time for the off-glide.

From the above, one sees that many factors enter into the timing of a diphthong. It is advisable to listen thoughtfully to the best Italian singers to get a sure sense of what is possible and what is beautiful.

One can be grateful that occasionally a composer chooses to separate the vowels of a diphthong into two syllables, showing us exactly how it should be sung. Splitting a diphthong in that way is never acceptable in English, but Italian composers do it to remove all doubt about their wishes.

Chapter 7: How Words Link

Italian words that are logically linked to each other in a phrase or a sentence are normally spoken in a *legato*, continuous utterance. Words that are spoken in a continuous way constitute a BREATH GROUP and sound like a long compound word. A narrow IPA transcription might show a breath group as a single word, but it would be confusing to interpret:

> /dɑlːlasuapaːtʃelamiadipɛnde/
> *Dalla sua pace la mia dipende...*
> My peace of mind depends on hers... (from *Don Giovanni*)

 Track 50

Listening to Italians speak, one cannot hear where one word ends and the next begins. Words even link over commas and other punctuation marks, much more often than in English. Words are spoken separately only for the sake of emphasis or unusual clarity, as when making details clear in a telephone conversation. This differs from English, in which breath groups are normally shorter and word separations are more numerous.

In Chapter 3 we explained various ways that written words may change when they are in the context of other words, for example, by elision, compounding, truncation and linking. The changes explained in this chapter include the subtle ones that are not shown by the orthography.

Canepàri uses the word *fonosillaba* /fonosilːlaba/ to describe sounds from two separate words that merge into a single audible syllable. When you read below about the final sound of a word being joined to the initial sound of the next word, it may be helpful to remember the concept of a PHONOSYLLABLE.

Consonant-to-Consonant Links

Linking from one consonant to another is generally easy in Italian. Links occur only after L, M, N or R: *il giovane* (the young man); *amiam per sempre* (let's love forever); *con lei* (with her). Just be sure that no extra vowel sound turns up unintentionally, changing, for instance, *con lei* (with her) into *con-a lei* (wrong).

If two identical consonants are linked, as the two L's in *il libro* (the book), they are sung *legato*, but an audible breath impulse makes the second L clear. If the two syllables are sung on different pitches, the consonant must be heard on both pitches. Neither one can be left out.

We have seen English examples of geminations, such as "slim man," "fine name," and others. Practice singing these Italian examples, with and without a pitch change between the linked consonants:

sul lago	/sulːlaːgo/	on the lake
andiam, mio bene	/andjamːmio bɛːne/	let's go, my dear
con noi	/konːnoi/	with us
per rabbia	/perːrabːbja/	for rage

Consonant-to-Vowel Links

Linking a final consonant to an initial vowel is somewhat less natural for English speakers. We do it constantly in relaxed speech, but we tend to separate words when we are speaking carefully. We may need reminders to sing and speak *legato* in Italian.

A final L, M, N or R links with the vowel that follows it with no gap between. In singing, the consonant and vowel may both be sung on the same pitch, forming a new phonosyllable (providing that this is vocally comfortable). In these examples the phonosyllable is underlined. (IPA does not usually show syllabication, but in special cases the division between syllables is indicated by a period, as in these examples.)

 Track 51

L: fata<u>l erro</u>re	/fa.ta:.ler:.ro:.re/	fatal mistake
M: andia<u>m insie</u>m	/an.dja:.min.sjɛm/	let's go together
N: no<u>n ha</u>	/no.na/	does not have
co<u>n altri</u>	/ko.nal.tri/	with others
i<u>n amore</u>	/i.na.mo:.re/	in love
R: (In linking to a vowel, a final Trill R changes to a Tap R /ɾ/.)		
o<u>r ora</u>	/o.ɾo:.ra/	right this minute

Vowel-to-Identical-Vowel Links

Linking from one vowel to another is a simple matter if each one is on a separate pitch. Even if they are identical vowels, like the A's in *mia anima* (my soul), the fact of singing them on different pitches makes the meaning clear.

If there is no pitch change between identical linked vowels, the composer usually writes only one note for them. They are sung as one phonosyllable. (If there is a particular interpretive point to be made, the singer may emphasize the second vowel with a slight breath impulse.) Vowels that are linked in this way are sung as long vowels if followed by a single consonant, even if both vowels are unstressed. In these examples, the linking of two unstressed short vowels produces a long vowel because they are followed by a single consonant.

guard<u>a ade</u>sso	/gwar.da:.dɛs:.so/	look now
molt<u>o one</u>sto	/mol.to:.nɛ.sto/	very virtuous
la fest<u>a ha</u> fin	/la fɛ.sta:.fin/	the holiday ends

Vowel-to-Contrasting-Vowel Links

If a stressed vowel must be linked to another stressed vowel, for instance, *piú alto* (higher), the two vowels form separate syllables. In music, they will usually have separate notes. They are sung *legato*, with no loss of clarity.

If only one of the vowels is stressed, or neither is stressed, the composer may either give them separate notes or merge the vowels together into one phonosyllable. A technical word for this merging process is synalepha, described in Chapter 1. It occurs often in Italian and Spanish but not in English, French or German.

In Italian arias it often seems that the lyric has more syllables than there are notes of music. To make the words fit, one must use synalepha to combine two written syllables into one phonosyllable. Even consecutive vowels separated by a punctuation mark may combine in a synalepha. But if there is a consonant between the vowels, they cannot merge. (When learning new music, it pays to check the distribution of syllables carefully. Engravers, even Italian engravers, often make mistakes in matching syllables to notes.)

The new phonosyllable contains a diphthong with two, three or four elements, including vowels and semivowels. Sometimes the note value is so short that there is barely enough time to articulate all of the elements. Otherwise, the singer has to decide which of the vowels is the main one that will be sustained for the length of the syllable, just as in normal diphthongs.

Some simple principles help us decide the main vowel in almost all cases of synalepha.

> a) A semivowel or the off-glide of a diphthong cannot be the main vowel.
>
> b) A vowel that is stressed in its word will be the main vowel in a synalepha. (Ex.: *prende ogni*, takes every). This may include a one- syllable word that is stressed in the phrase for whatever reason. (Ex.: *è*, is.) It does not include a word that is naturally unstressed in the phrase, such as the article *uno, una*.
>
> c) Choosing between two unstressed vowels, prolong the one that is underlined in this chart.[1]

> Most Italian poems have either 7 or 11 syllables per line; other syllable counts are less common. To scan a poem correctly we must know how the vowels combine. In the following lines, written by an anonymous woman in the late 1200s, each line has 11 syllables. Can you count them?
>
> *A la stagion che il mondo foglia e fiora*
> *accresce gioia a tutt'i fini amanti. . .*
> (In the season when the earth puts out leaves and flowers, the joy of all gentle lovers increases. . .)
>
> Can you identify the syllables that must be combined into diphthongs to clarify the meter? (Answers: *"che il," "-glia e," "-ia a," -ni a-."*)
>
> What is the minimum number of notes a composer could use to set each of the above lines to music? (Answer: 11.) Of course, the composer might use more notes in slurs or by breaking up the diphthongs, according to taste.

Second Vowel

		A	E	I	O	U
F i r s t V o w e l	**A**	———	variable	a̯ i	a̯ o	a̯ u
	E	e̯ a	———	e̯ i	variable	e̯ u
	I	i̯ a	i̯ e	———	i̯ o	i̯ u
	O	o̯ a	o̯ e	o̯ i	———	o̯ u

Notice that /i/ is never the main vowel of a synalepha. If it is the first of two vowels, it makes sense to transcribe it as /j/. Only a few words end in U, and they are strong words, such as *fu* (was) and *giù* (down), which are naturally stressed in a synalepha.

Given that we are practicing an art and not a science, there can be many variables in musical situations, and there can be disagreements among Italians about the most beautiful way to perform a particular phrase. Nevertheless, the principles just explained will answer nearly all questions about synalepha. Many examples are found in the musical phrases quoted in Chapters 4 and 5.

---

[1] Thanks to Dr. René Aravena for the concept of this chart.

Even when three or four vowel letters appear in a synalepha, exactly the same method will serve to select one main vowel. That means: eliminate semivowels and off-glides of diphthongs; select a vowel that is stressed in the word or phrase; in the absence of a stressed vowel, use the chart above. In a majority of cases the second of the three or four vowels is the main one.

When a synalepha occurs with a group of slurred notes, it behaves just like other diphthongs: the main vowel is prolonged. The off-glide is sung on the last one or two of the slurred notes, just like the off-glide of a true diphthong.

During the learning process, it can be helpful to assign rhythmic values to the vowels in a synalepha so as to clarify which vowel is the main one and which must be sung as quickly as possible. But eventually the vowels must flow naturally as they do in speech. If the composer wanted the vowels to sound like separate notes, they would be written that way.

Vowel-to-Consonant Links

Since most words end in vowels and most words begin with consonants, the most common link of all is from final vowel to initial consonant. This results in a smooth legato with open syllables following each other in sequence.

 Track 52

Italian speech has a peculiarity that some singers like to employ: gemination of an initial consonant after a short word that ends in a vowel. Because this gemination occurs only between two words, the Italian term for it is *cogeminazione* /kodʒeminatsjoːne/. Authors have used various terms in English, but we will call this procedure COGEMINATION.

Cogemination is a normal part of daily speech, and some singers use it to add emphasis and expression to a lyric. The naturalness of cogemination is evident in a number of expressions that are written either as phrases or as single words in modern Italian, e.g., *chi sà? chissà?* (who knows?), *se bene, sebbene* (even if). Such word combinations are pronounced the same, whether written as one word or two.

Using cogemination is always optional, not essential; it does not make a singer sound any more or any less Italian. (If you decide to leave this for later study, you may skip the rest of this discussion and go to the next topic.) But if you decide to use it, it must be used correctly, and that is why it is discussed here.

Only certain words cause cogemination. The dictionaries of both Zingarelli and Canepàri show these words with an asterisk. An asterisk after the phonetics means that the initial consonant of the next word may (optionally) be doubled, as for instance:

se /se*/ (if).

This confirms the example above, in which *se bene* is spoken, and even written, with cogemination.

An asterisk before the phonetics means that the initial consonant of the word itself should always be doubled if preceded by a vowel, as for instance:

sciolto /*ʃɔlto/ (loosened).

The latter case is not considered cogemination, but merely the correct way of saying certain consonants—GLI, GN, soft SC, and Z—when they are between two vowels.

The following examples show some typical words and expressions with textual doubling. The list cannot possibly be complete, but it shows the kinds of words that cause textual doubling: many one-syllable words, a few two-syllable prepositions and conjunctions; and words that end with a stressed vowel.

Adverbs: *che, cosí, già, giú, là, lí, no, piú, qua, qui, sí, su*

che bella	/keb:bɛl:la/	what a beauty
cosí fan tutte	/kozif:fan tut:te/	so do all women
piú chiaro	/pjuk:kja:ro/	brighter

Conjunctions: *che, e, ma, né, o, se*

e pure, eppure	/ep:pu:re/	and yet
ma geloso	/mad:dʒelo:zo/	but jealous
o crema	/ok:krɛ:ma/	or cream

Prepositions: *a, fra, tra, su*

a quando	/ak:kwando/	until when?
su pietra	/sup:pjɛ:tra/	on stone

Pronouns (a few): *chi, che, ciò, tu*

chi vuol	/kiv:vwɔl/	who wants
tu capisci	/tuk:kapiʃ:ʃi/	you understand

Verbs: *dà, do, è, fa, fu, ha, ho, può, sa, so, sta, sto, va,* verbs ending in *-à, -ò*

dà pace	/dap:pa:tʃe/	gives peace
è bella	/ɛb:bɛl:la/	she is beautiful
fa caldo	/fak:kaldo/	it is hot weather
ho fame	/ɔf:fa:me/	I am hungry
può darsi	/pwɔd:darsi/	it may happen
sarò (starò) vicino	/sarɔv:vitʃi:no/	I shall be near
sto fermo	/stɔf:fɛrmo/	I am determined

Some other one-syllable words:

re Carlo	/rek:karlo/	King Carlo
tre città	/tret:tʃit:ta/	three cities

Articles and most pronouns do not cause cogemination, and there are many other common words that do not, including: *da* (from), *di* (of), *o* (vocative, as in "oh, mother!").

Elision

The final vowel of a word may sometimes be omitted when the following word begins with a vowel. This omission, called an elision, is indicated by an apostrophe. In Italian grammar some elisions are required, such as these: Track 53

l'amico (= lo amico)	/lami:ko/	the friend
un'opera d'arte (= una opera di arte)	/unɔ:pera darte/	a work of art

Other elisions are optional, such as the following:

dell'onde (= delle onde)	/delːˈonde/	of the waves
dovrebb'essere (= dovrebbe essere)	/dovrˈebːbˈesːsere/	ought to be

Two words that are joined by an apostrophe are pronounced without any interruption, just as if they were one word. Elision may result in two stressed syllables being adjacent to each other, an unusual situation in Italian. An example of this was given in Chapter 3, page 26.

The Italian word *elisione* means both elision and synalepha.

Truncation

Italians often drop the final vowel of a word if they feel that this will result in a better rhythm. The whole final syllable or even two syllables may be dropped in some circumstances. This omission is called in Italian *troncamento* /tronkamento/, or in English, truncation. Poets often shorten words to fit them into a line with a predetermined number of syllables.

A word may be truncated only if the remaining part ends with one of the sustainable voiced consonants, L, M, N or R. A word such as *affetto*, for instance, cannot be truncated because the remaining part would end with T. No apostrophe is used. Again, the result can be two stressed syllables sung consecutively.

alfin respiro (=alfine respiro)	/alfin respiːro/	at last I am breathing
andiam (=andiamo)	/andjam/	let's go
caro mio ben (=bene)	/kaːro mio bɛn/	dear my good
bell'idol (=bello idolo)	/bɛlːliːdol/	beautiful idol
v'entrar (=vi entrarono)	/ventrar/	they entered here

Notice that in most of these cases the stressed syllable contains a vowel that is normally long, for instance, /ɛː/ in /bɛːne/. When the word is truncated, the final consonant steals time away from the vowel.

By far the most common *troncamento* is cutting off the -E of the infinitive ending -RE. If this occurs before a silence or before a consonant, the tap /ɾ/ changes to a trill /r/.

il mio cantar (cantare)	/mio kantar/	my singing
baciar potrò (baciare)	/batʃaːr potrɔː/	to kiss I will be able

If final -RE changes to -R before a vowel, the R is a tap, not a trill, and is attached to the following vowel.

amor eterno (amore)	/amo.retɛrno/	eternal love

Chapter 8: Singing Italian in an Aria

Having studied all of the phonetic elements that enter into Italian singing, it is time to see how they work together. This chapter analyzes some excerpts from two famous soprano arias, detailing exactly what happens, note by note.

As we stated at the beginning of this book, "if we want to sing like native Italians, we have to know and understand many things that an Italian takes for granted." Since you have been practicing Italian diction, many things come automatically to you, but there may still be doubtful areas that cause you some vocal insecurity. Often an apparent problem of vocal technique will disappear when the singer understands clearly what vowel and consonant sounds to sing.

In all of the following examples it should be understood that:
1) every vowel, semivowel and consonant must be heard, none omitted;

2) the connections between the sounds must be made smoothly, but without gaps and without extra sounds intruding; and

3) the final goal is *communication* achieved with comfort and flexibility, rather than strictness and rigidity.

In the analyses given here, the syllables are numbered for easy reference. By reading down the syllable column, you can easily find exactly what phonetic sounds to sing on each note.

A Mozart Sample

Zerlina's aria, *"Batti, batti, o bel Masetto,"* from *Don Giovanni*, Act I.

This example shows a complete text of the aria, omitting the repetitions, demonstrating many normal features as well as others that are unusual.

Mozart's melodies sometimes go against the correct word accents (in this excerpt, c<u>o</u>me, star<u>ò</u> and agnell<u>í</u>na). Mozart spoke Italian perfectly, and he knew that the singers whom he trained would not put false accents on c<u>o</u>me, star<u>ò</u>, <u>agnellina</u>, or unimportant words like *la* or *le*.

Beat, beat, o handsome Masetto, your poor Zerlina,

1. /bat/   quick /b/, short /a/, /t/ stops the tone for ¼ to ⅓ of the beat
2. /ti/   /t/ releases (no aspiration), pure /i/
3. /bat/   as before
4. /tio/   /t/ releases, quick /i/, pure /o/
5. /bɛl/   quick /b/, pure /ɛ/, expressive /l/ (less than ¹⁄₁₆ value)
6. /ma/   quick /m/, pure /a/
7. /zet/   quick /z/, pure /e/, /t/ stops the tone for ¼-⅓ of the note
8. /to/   /t/ releases, pure /o/, shortened to take breath
9. /la/   quick /l/, pure /a/
10. /tua/   quick /t/, pure /u/, quick /a/ at the end of the note
11. /pɔː/   quick /p/, pure /ɔː/
12. /ve/   quick /v/ (on pitch!), pure /e/
13. /rad/   tap R, pure /a/, /d/ fills the last ¼-⅓ of the note
14. /dzer/   /d/ releases, quick /z/, pure /e/, trill R fills the last ¼-⅓ of the note
15. /liː/   quick /l/, pure /iː/
16. /na/   quick /n/, pure /a/ (breath)

sta - rò   qui   co-me a-gnel - li - na   le   tue   bot - te ad a - spet - tar.
                   20   25   30

I shall be here like a lamb, your blows to await.

17.   /staː/   quick /st/, pure /aː/
18.   /rɔ/   tap R, pure /ɔ/
19.   /kwiː/   quick /kw/, pure /i/
20.   /koː/   quick /k/, pure /o/
21.   /meaɲ/   *three possibilities:*
            (1) as written (difficult and somewhat awkward): quick /m/,
                quick /e/, pure /a/, /ɲ/ fills the last ¼-⅓ of the note;
            (2) omit /e/, singing *com'agnellina*;
            (3) sing /me/ as a grace-note ahead of the beat on the pitch of
                the preceding syllable (normally, one should avoid adding
                an extra note in this way)
22.   /ɲel/   /ɲ/ releases, pure /e/, /l/ fills the last ¼-⅓ of the note
23.   /liː/   /l/ releases, pure /iː/
24.   /na/   quick /n/, pure /a/ (breath?)
25.   /le/   quick /l/, pure /e/ (not stressed!)
26.   /tṳe/   quick /t/, pure /u/, quick /e/ at the end of the note
27.   /bɔt/   quick /b/, pure /ɔ/, /t/ stops the tone for ¼-⅓ of the note
28.   /te/   quick /t/, quick /e/ (ignore the slur)
29.   /a/   pure /a/ (on the pitch c)
30.   /da/   quick /d/, pure /a/
31.   /spet/   quick /sp/, pure /e/, /t/ stops the tone for ¼-⅓ of the note
32.   /tar/   /t/ releases, pure /a/, trill R fills the last ¼-⅓ of the beat

Continuing Zerlina's aria:

La - scie - rò   stra - ziar mi il   cri - ne,
                         5

I will let you pull my hair,

1.   /laʃ/   quick /l/, short /a/, /ʃ/ fills ¼-⅓ of the note
2.   /ʃe/   /ʃ/ releases, pure /e/
3.   /rɔ/   tap R, /ɔ/ shortened because next syllable begins early
4.   /strat/   quick /st/ and trill R before the beat, /a/ on the beat, /t/ stop
5.   /tsjar/   /t/ releases, quick /s/, quick /j/, pure /a/, trill R fills the note
6.   /miːl/   quick /m/, pure /iː/, /l/ fills the note
7.   /kriː/   quick /r/, trill /r/, pure /i/
8.   /ne/   quick n, pure /e/

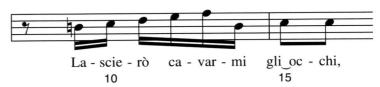

La - scie - rò   ca - var - mi   gli‿oc - chi,
                10   15
I will let you dig out my eyes,

9. /la/   quick /l/, pure /a/ (*lascierò*, as before)
10. /ʃe/   /ʃ/ releases, pure /e/
11. /rɔː/   tap R, pure /ɔː/
12. /ka/   quick /k/, pure /a/
13. /var/   quick /v/, short /a/, trill R fills ¼-⅓ of the note
14. /miʎ/   quick /m/, pure /i/, /ʎ/ fills ¼-⅓ of the note
15. /ʎɔk/   /ʎ/ releases, quick /ɔ/, /k/ stops the tone
16. /ki/   /k/ releases, quick /i/ (breath)

e__ le__   ca - re tue__ ma - ni - ne lie - ta__   poi__ sa - prò__ ba - ciar,
            20   25   30
and your dear hands, happily then I will be able to kiss.

17. /e/   pure /e/
18. /le/   quick /l/, pure /e/
19. /kaː/   quick /k/, pure /aː/, silence (without breath)
20. /re/   tap /r/, pure /e/ (careful: do not accent this syllable)
21. /tu/   quick /t/, pure /u/ (ignore the slur)
22. /e/   pure /e/
23. /ma/   quick /m/, pure /a/
24. /niː/   quick /n/, pure /i/, silence (without breath)
25. /ne/   quick /n/, pure /e/ (no accent!)
26. /ljɛː/   quick /l/, semivowel /j/, /ɛː/
27. /ta/   quick /t/, pure /a/
28. /pɔ/   quick /p/, pure /ɔ/ (ignore the slur)
29. /i/   pure /i/ (breath)
30. /sa/   quick /s/, pure /a/ (the next syllable begins early)
31. /prɔ/   quick /p/ and trill R ahead of the note, pure /O/
32. /ba/   quick /b/, pure /a/
33. /tʃar/   quick /tʃ/, pure /a/ slurred on two 8ths, trill R on third 8th, breath

Continuing Zerlina's aria:

Ah,   lo   ve - do,   non   hai   co - re,
                                         5
Ah, I see it; you don't have the heart /to beat me/...

1. /aː/   pure /aː/
2. /lo/   quick /l/, pure /o/
3. /veː/   quick /v/, pure /eː/ slurred on two notes
4. /do/   quick /d/, pure /o/
5. /noː/   quick /n/, pure /oː/
6. /nai/   quick /n/, pure /a/, quick /i/ at the end of the note
7. /kɔː/   quick /k/, pure /ɔː/
8. /re/   tap R, pure /e/

Finishing Zerlina's aria, from measure 64:

Peace, o my life! In contentedness and happiness,

1.   /paː   /quick /p/, pure /aː/ slurred on two notes
2.   /tʃeo/   quick /tʃ/, pure /e/, quick /oː/
3.   /viː/   quick /v/, pure /iː/ slurred on two notes
4.   /ta/   quick /t/, pure /a/
5.   /miː/   quick /m/, pure /iː/
6.   /a/   pure /a/, breath
7.   /in/   pure /i/ slurred, /n/ fills ¼-⅓ of the second note
8.   /kon/   quick /k/, pure /oː/ slurred, /n/ fills ¼-⅓ of the note
9.   /tɛn/   quick /t/, pure /ɛ/, /n/ fills ¼-⅓ of the second note
10. /toe/   quick /t/, pure /o/, quick /e/ at the end of the note
11. /dal/   quick /d/, pure /a/ slurred, /l/ fills ¼-⅓ of the second note
12. /le/   /l/ releases, pure /e/ (the next syllable begins early)
13. /griː/   quick /g/, trill R (ahead of the note), pure /iː/ slurred
14. /a/   pure /a/ (breath?)

not - te e dì — vo - gliam — pas - sar, ———
15   20

night and day we want to spend.

15. /nɔt/   quick /n/, pure /ɔ/, /t/ stops the second note
16. /teː/   /t/ releases, pure /eː/
17. /diː/   quick /d/, pure /iː/ slurred
18. /voʎ/   quick /v/, pure /oː/, /ʎ/ fills ¼-⅓ of the note
19. /ʎam/   /ʎ/ releases, pure /a/, /m/ fills ¼-⅓ of the second note
20. /pas/   quick /p/, pure /a/, /s/ fills ¼-⅓ of the note
21. /sar/   /s/ releases, pure /a/, trill R

A Puccini Sample

Musetta's aria, *"Quando me'n vo,"* from *La Bohème*, Act II.

An interesting feature of this excerpt is that the initial sounds of certain syllables begin a considerable length of time before the proper time for the note to sound. This happens because the vowel must sound on the rhythmic beat, even if a group of consonants comes ahead of the beat.

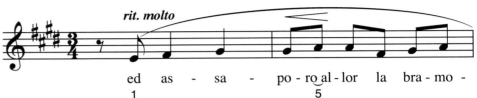

ed   as - sa -   po - ro al - lor   la   bra - mo -
1   5

"...and I savor then the subtle yearning that from the eyes escapes...

sia   sot - til,——   che   da   gl'oc - chi tra - spi - ra
10   15   19

1	/e/	pure, closed vowel
2	/das/	quick /d/ on beat 2, pure /a/, /s/ fills the last ¼-⅓ of the beat
3.	/a/	pure vowel
4.	/poː/	quick, unaspirated /p/, pure, closed /o/
5.	/ɾo‿al/	tap R, short /o/ connects to longer /a/, /l/ on last ¼ of the note
6.	/lor/	quick /l/, pure /o/, trill R fills about ¼-⅓ of the beat
7.	/la/	quick /l/, pure /a/, shortened because *next syllable begins early*
8.	/bra/	quick /b/ and trill R sung (on G♯) ahead of beat 3, pure /a/
9.	/mo/	quick /m/, pure /o/, shortened because of grace notes
10.	/zia/	*ahead of the barline*, quick /z/, pure /i/ on grace notes, /i/ continues on beat 1, quick /a/ at the end of the note.
11.	/sot/	quick /s/, pure /o/, /t/ stops the tone for ¼-⅓ of the beat
12.	/til/	/t/ releases (no aspiration), pure /i/ on two notes, /l/ fills about ¼-⅓ of the F♯, obligatory breath.
13.	/ke/	quick /k/, pure /e/
14.	/daʎ/	quick /d/, short /a/, /ʎ/ fills the last ¼-⅓ of the note
15.	/ʎɔk/	/ʎ/ releases (no /i/ is heard), /ɔ/ on two notes, /k/ stops the tone for about ¼-⅓ of the second note.
16.	/ki/	quick /k/, pure /i/, shortened because next syllable begins early
17.	/tras/	quick /t/ and trill R sung (on e) ahead of the half-beat, /a/ on the half- beat, quick /s/ at the end of the note
18.	/piː/	quick /p/, long, pure /i/
19.	/ra/	tap R, pure /a/

Of course, all of these events occur within about ten seconds, and an Italian-speaking singer does most of them automatically.

A Final Checklist

☑ Have you worked with your personal Italian dictionary enough to learn how it shows pronunciations? Do you know the differences between that dictionary's phonetic style and the style used in this book? No two dictionaries show pronunciations in identical ways, but the areas of difference need not be confusing if you take time to sort them out.

☑ Do you trill every R or RR that deserves to be trilled, taking the necessary time and using the appropriate breath energy? (Your vocal tone will benefit if you do.) Do you voice the R's, that is, sing them?

☑ Do you tap a single R between vowels with the tip of your tongue and never allow an American R to creep in?

☑ Do you elongate every double consonant, subtracting the necessary time from the preceding vowel and note? Do you know that medial Z, GLI, GN, and soft SC should be sung as if they were double?

☑ Do you allow silence when a voiceless stop consonant is geminated, as in *bocca*?

☑ Are you sure that single consonants between notes are *not* elongated and that the preceding vowels are as long as the music allows?

☑ Do you pronounce every consonant in a cluster, taking enough time for those that need time? Do you voice S before another voiced consonant, as in *sgelo*?

☑ Do you pronounce the voiceless stops without aspirating them? Do you remember the "dental" consonants and articulate them forward, against the upper teeth?

☑ Do you remember to keep the tongue tip down for GLI and GN?

☑ Do you keep every vowel quality pure for as long as it should be, with no accidental, unintentional diphthongs? Are you especially careful with stressed, closed /e/ and /o/?

☑ Have you checked all stressed E's and O's to be sure which are closed and which are open?

☑ Do you keep vowels pure in unstressed syllables? (Trap: words that look like English words but have completely different vowel sounds: *opera, passione, contento, infinito, salata,* etc.)

☑ Is your /i/ always pure, never /ɪ/ or /ɪə/, especially in initial syllables such as *il-, im-,* or *-in,* and within a word, before /l/ and /r/?

☑ When one syllable contains two or more vowels, do you sing them with pure and clear vowel qualities? Do you change from one to another quickly, without an unnecessary gliding sound, either /j/ or /w/?

☑ Especially in recitative, but whenever the musical rhythm resembles speech rhythm, are you aware of long vowels and keeping the illusion of speech rhythm in your singing?

In Closing

If all of the points above have become habits for you– *bravo!* It is time for the author to wish you *molto piacere e successo*, much pleasure and success in singing Italian.

Part 3: Supplements

Alphabetical Key

Spellings are shown in upper-case and are arranged alphabetically.
<u>A spelling may be associated with more than one IPA symbol.</u>

Spelling	IPA	Page
A, À	/a/	37
A (stressed, before a single consonant)	/aː/	37
B	/b/	60
BB	/bːb/	60
C (before A, O, U, H, R or L)	/k/	63
C (in syllables CE, CI)	/tʃ/	47, 72
CC (before A, O, U or H)	/kːk/	47, 63
CC (before E, I)	/tːtʃ/	47, 72
CH (before E, I)	/k/	47, 63
CCH (before E, I)	/kːk/	47, 63
CI (before A, O, U)	/tʃ/	47, 72
CCI (before A, O, U)	/tːtʃ/	47, 72
CIE	/tʃɛ/	73
CQU	/kːkw/	63
D	/d/	62
DD	/dːd/	62
E (in all unstressed and some stressed syllables), É	/e/	34
E (in some stressed syllables, before a single consonant)	/eː/	34
E (in some stressed syllables)	/ɛ/	35
E (in some stressed syllables, before a single consonant)	/ɛː/	35
F	/f/	65
FF	/fːf/	65
G (before A, O, U, H, R or L)	/g/	64
G (in syllables GE, GI)	/dʒ/	73
GG (before A, O, U, H, R or L)	/gːg/	64
GG (before E, I)	/dːdʒ/	73

GH (before E,.I)	/g/	65
GGH (before E, I)	/gːg/	65
GI (before A, O, U)	/dʒ/	74
GGI (before A, O, U)	/dːdʒ/	74
GLI (as a syllable, in most words, initially)	/ʎi/	55
GLI (as a syllable, in most words, medially)	/ʎːʎi/	55
GLI (as a syllable, in a few words)	/gli/	55
GLI (before another vowel in the same syllable, initially)	/ʎ/	55
GLI (before another vowel in the same syllable, medially)	/ʎːʎ/	55
GN (initially)	/ɲ/	51, 52
GN (medially)	/ɲːɲ/	51, 52
H	silent	47
I, Í	/i/	32
I (stressed, before a single consonant)	/iː/	32
I (unstressed, before another vowel)	/j/	32, 42
I (after C, G or SC and before another vowel)	silent	32, 47
II	/iː/	33
J (obsolete)	/j/	32, 42
L (see GLI, above)	/l/	54
LL	/lːl/	54
M	/m/	50
MM	/mːm/	50
N (see GN, above)	/n/	51
N (before /g/ or /k/)	/ŋ/	51, 53
NN	/nːn/	51
O (in all unstressed and some stressed syllables)	/o/	39
O (in some stressed syllables, before a single consonant)	/oː/	39
O (in some stressed syllables), Ò	/ɔ/	40
O (in some stressed syllables, before a single consonant)	/ɔː/	40
Ò	/ɔ/	40

P	/p/	59
PP	/pːp/	59
QU	/kw/	63
R (between two vowels)	/ɾ/	58
R (final, before a word beginning with a vowel)	/ɾ/	58
R (in all other situations)	/r/	58
RR	/rːr/	58
S (between two vowels or before a voiced consonant/	/z/	68
S (otherwise)	/s/	67
SC (before A, O, U or H)	/sk/	47
SC (before E or I, initially)	/ʃ/	69
SC (before E or I, medially)	/ʃːʃ/	69
SCH (before E or I)	/sk/	47
SCI (before A, O or U, initially)	/ʃ/	47, 69
SCI (before A, O or U, medially)	/ʃːʃ/	47, 69
SS	/sːs/	67
T	/t/	61
TT	/tːt/	61
U, Ú	/u/	38
U (stressed, before a single consonant)	/uː/	38
U (unstressed, before another vowel)	/w/	43
V	/v/	66
VV	/vːv/	66
W	/v/	66
X	/ks/	64
Z (use a dictionary)	/ts/ or /dz/	70, 71
ZZ (use a dictionary)	/tːts/, /dːdz/	70, 71

E and O: Closed or Open?

The variable pronunciations of E and of O are among the most perplexing aspects of Italian, not just for foreigners but for Italians who want to improve their own speech. Books about standard Italian speech devote many pages to this dilemma.

There are several reasons for the difficulties concerning closed and open vowels. First, local pronunciations differ; for example, *cielo* (sky, heaven) is /tʃɛːlo/ in standard Italian but /tʃeːlo/ in Neapolitan, and many words listed below have a non-standard pronunciation somewhere in Italy. Secondly, there are changes as time goes by: many words have a "modern" pronunciation with a closed E or O and a "traditional" one, used onstage or in classical poetry, with an open vowel. And it has always been true that the rules governing open and closed E and O are numerous and riddled with complicated exceptions.

This author has long had the habit of checking every occurrence of a stressed E or O in the dictionary to see whether it should be closed or open. However, this book offers some guidance for those who do not have dictionaries that provide sufficient details about pronunciations. Also, it may be easier to memorize correct pronunciations if you know the following typical patterns. It is best to regard them as patterns of use, not as rules.

The following material is drawn largely from the much more detailed discussion and syllable lists found in Canepàri's *Dizionario,* pages 61–71. It may be comforting to know that Canepàri counsels his Italian readers: "For what is following, one is strongly advised to proceed calmly, with many repetitions, reflecting adequately on each point, without haste, and always considering everything, whether in general or in particular."

E: /e/ or /ɛ/?

The difference between /e/ and /ɛ/ is phonemic in Italian, as shown by minimal word pairs like those listed here. (Both lists are standard Italian. The differences in meaning depend solely on the pronunciation of the stressed vowel.)

e /e/, and	è /ɛ/, and
l'accetta /atːtʃetːta/, hatchet	l'accetta /atːtʃɛtːta/, accepts it
l'arena /areːna/, sand	l'arena /arɛːna/, arena
credo /kreːdo/, I believe	il credo /krɛːdo/, creed
dette /detːte/, said (from *dire*)	dette /dɛtːte/, gave (from *dare*)
l'esca /eska/, bait, attraction	esca /ɛska/, may go out (*uscire*)
esse /esːse/, they	esse /ɛsːse/, letter S
la legge /ledːdʒe/, law	legge /lɛdːdʒe/, reads
mesto /mesto/, stir (*mestare*)	mesto /mɛsto/, sad
mezzo /metːtso/, ready to spoil	mezzo /mɛdːdzo/, middle, medium, half
la pesca /peska/, fishing	la pesca /pɛska/, peach
il re /re/, king	il re /rɛ/, note above *do*
la tema /teːma/, fear	il tema /tɛːma/, theme
venti /venti/, twenty	i venti /vɛnti/, winds

E is pronounced closed /e/ in all unstressed syllables and in these cases:
- in monosyllables, except *tè* (tea) and *è* and *re* in the above list:

| me, te, se | /me te se/ | me, you, if |

- in the demonstrative pronouns *codesto* (this), *quello* (that), *questo* (that):

| quello[1] | /kwelːlo/ | that |

- in the infinitive ending *-ere* and in the stressed verb endings *-ea, -eano, -ei* (but not *-rei*), *-emmo, -érono, -esse, -éssero, -essi, -éssimo, -este, -esti, -ete, -etti, -éttero, -eva, -évano, -evi, -evo, -remmo, -remo, -rete*:

sapete	/sapeːte/	you know
vedere, vederla	/vedeːɾe vedeːɾla/	to see, to see her
se l'avessimo	/se lavesːsimo/	if we had it

- in the suffixes *-eccio, -éfice, -eggio, -egno, -esco, -ese, -esimo* (except after numbers), *-essa* (used to make a noun feminine), *-eta, -ete, -eto, -évole, -ezza, -mento* (as a suffix, not in the root of the word):

aragonese	/aragoneːze/	from Aragon
cristianesimo	/kristjaneːzimo/	Christianity
il conte, la contessa	/konte kontesːsa/	count, countess
il tradimento	/tradimento/	betrayal

- in the diminutive or collective suffix *-etta, -etto*:

allegretto	/alːlegretːto/	little, a bit fast
duetto	/duetːto/	duet
violetta, Violetta	/violetːta/	violet, operatic role

- in *mente* and the common suffix *-mente*:

| la mente | /mente/ | mind |
| finalmente | /finalmente/ | finally |

E is pronounced open /ɛ/ in stressed syllables in these cases:
- nearly always, in the combination IE and in some words that have alternative spellings with E or IE:

| pieno | /pjɛːno/ | full |
| altero, altiero | /altɛːɾo altjɛːɾo/ | haughty |

- usually, when another vowel follows it immediately:

| lei, Lei | /lɛːi/ | she, you (polite) |
| dea, dei | /dɛːa dɛːi/ | goddess, gods |

(but not the preposition *dei* /dei/, of the)

| reo | /rɛːo/ | guilty |

(but verb endings in *-ea* or *-eano* have the closed E)

---

[1]Some words have endings to show gender and number. In the word lists that follow, a pronoun or adjective ending in *-o* may also end in *-a, -e,* or *-i.* A noun or adjective ending in *-e* has a plural form that ends in *-i.* The quality of the stressed vowel remains the same.

- usually, in the third-from-last (antepenultimate) syllable, but with many exceptions:

  il medico   /mɛːdiko/   doctor

  ventesimo   /ventɛːzimo/   twentieth
  (but 3rd person plural verbs, like *vedono*, have the closed E)

- in the diminutive suffix -*ɛllo*:

  violoncello   /violontʃɛlːlo/   little, cello (little viol)
  (but not in the diminutive -*etto*, or in the pronoun *quello*)

- in these verb endings:-*ɛndo* (gerund),-*ɛnte* (but not -*mente*), -*ɛnse*, *ɛnza*, -*ɛro* (in words of three or more syllables), -*ɛrrimo*, -*ɛtte*, -*ɛttero*, -*ɛtti*, -*ɛri*, -*rɛbbe*, -*rɛbbero*.

  avendo   /avɛndo/   having (gerund)

  vorrei   /vorːrɛi/   I would like

- in these suffixes (except if they are added to the verbs *tenere, venire*, and their derivatives): -*ɛnne*, -*ɛnni*, -*ɛnnio*.

  ventenni   /ventɛnːni/   twenty-year periods
  (but *tenni* /tenːni/, I kept)

- in these suffixes: -*ɛma*, -*ɛndine*, -*ɛno* (ethnic adj.), -*ɛsimo* (after numbers), -*ɛstre*, -*ɛstro*, - *ɛvolo*, -*ɛzio*.

  nazareno   /nadːdzarɛːno/   Nazarene

  trentesimo   /trentɛːzimo/   thirtieth

- in the spelling -*rr*- (but not necessarily other double consonants):

  la guerra   /gwɛrːra/   war

All of the discussion above has dealt with the phonemes /e/ and /ɛ/, because the author considers these both essential and sufficient for singing Italian. In narrow transcriptions of spoken Italian, Canepàri recognizes an intermediate E in some unstressed syllables. He shows this allophone with the non-standard symbol /ᴇ/ (small capital E).

O: /o/ or /ɔ/?

The difference between /o/ and /ɔ/ is phonemic in Italian, as shown by minimal word pairs like those listed here. (Again, both lists are standard Italian. The differences in meaning depend on the pronunciation of the stressed vowel.)

la botte /botːte/, barrel	le botte /bɔtːte/, blows
colto /kolto/, cultured	colto /kɔlto/, collected
i conservatori /konservatoːri/, politicians	i conservatori /konservatɔːri/, music schools
ora /oːra/, now	ora! /ɔːra/, pray!
lui pose /poːze/, he put (*porre*)	le pose /pɔːze/, attitudes
lui rose /roːze/, he gnawed (*rodere*)	le rose /rɔːze/, roses
scopo /skoːpo/, I sweep	lo scopo /skɔːpo/, aim, purpose
la torta /torta/, cake	torta /tɔrta/, twisted, wrung
la torre /torːre/, tower	torre /tɔrːre/, to take away (old form)
il volgo /volgo/, common people	volgo /vɔlgo/, I turn
il volto /volto/, face	volto /vɔlto/, turned

O is pronounced closed /o/ in all unstressed syllables and in these cases:
- in most monosyllables, including these: *con* (with), *lo, non, o* (or), *o!*:

o! non lo conosco	/o non lo konosko/	Oh, I don't know!

  (but see other monosyllables under /ɔ/)

- before GN:

ogni sogno	/oɲːɲi soɲːɲo/	every dream

- in the suffixes *-oio, -ondo, -one, -onte, -onzolo, -ore, -oso* (adjectives)

il farfallone	/farfalːloːne/	frivolous person
doloroso	/doloroːzo/	sad, painful

O is pronounced open /ɔ/ in stressed syllables in these cases:
- in *no* and in one syllable nouns and verbs:

do, ho, so	/dɔ ɔ sɔ/	I give, have, know
do, Po	/dɔ pɔ/	first note of the scale, river

- in the combination UO and in words that have alternative spellings with O or UO:

cuore, core	/kwɔːre kɔːre/	heart
buono, bono	/bwɔːno bɔːno/	good

  (but not before the suffix *-oso*:)

affettuoso	/afːfetːtuoːzo/	affectionate

- In the third-from-last (antepenultimate) syllable, with some exceptions:

l'opera	/ɔːpera/	opera
povero, -a	/pɔːvero pɔːvera/	poor

- When followed by another vowel or semivowel:

poi	/pɔi/	then
la gioia	/dʒɔːja/	joy

(but /o/ is closed in *noi* (we), *voi* (you), and *coi* (with the))

- When followed by a syllable that contains a semivowel:

gloria	/glɔːrja /	glory

- Before GLI /ʎ/:

voglio	/vɔʎːʎo/	I want
cogliere	/kɔʎːʎere/	to gather

(but /o/ is closed in *la moglie* (wife))

- At the end of a word, with stress indicated by an accent mark:

parlò	/parlɔ/	he spoke
parlerò	/parlerɔ/	I shall speak

- in the suffixes *-ɔccio, -ɔide, -ɔlo, -ɔsi* (medical terms), *-ɔtto,*
  -ɔttolo, -ɔzzo:

il giovanotto	/dʒovanɔtːto/	young man

All of the discussion above has dealt with the phonemes /o/ and /ɔ/, because the author considers these both essential and sufficient for singing Italian. In narrow transcriptions of spoken Italian, Canepàri recognizes an intermediate O in some unstressed syllables. He shows this allophone with the non-standard symbol /σ/ (lower-case Greek sigma).

Fratelli d'Italia  Track 55

Goffredo Mameli, 1847

Michele Novaro, 1847

Brothers of Italy, Italy has awakened; with the helmet of Scipio it is armed. Where is victory? May it bow its head to her (Italy), because God created it (victory) to serve as a slave to Rome.

This stirring anthem was written in the fall of 1847 by two young men in their 20's, both from Genoa, Goffredo Mameli /goffreːdo mameːli/ (1827–1849) and Michele Novaro /mikeːle novaːro/ (1822–1885). Within two months the song was sung by a crowd of 30,000 people in Genoa at a patriotic demonstration. The following years saw a series of wars for the liberation of Italy from the oppressive rule of foreign powers and, in central Italy, of the pope. This song inspired the patriots more than any other. In 1849 Pope Pius IX was driven out of Rome and a republic was declared. Mameli and other patriots rushed to defend it, but they were no match for the French soldiers who came to reinstate the pope. Mameli was wounded and died of gangrene.

When a free Italy was finally unified in 1870, it was a parliamentary monarchy. *"Fratelli d'Italia"* was too revolutionary in spirit for the conservative royalty, but the song was often sung as an unofficial patriotic song. This continued under Mussolini's fascism, which fell in 1945. The next year *"Fratelli d'Italia"* was chosen as the national anthem by the constitutional assembly that established the present Italian Republic. It is sometimes known as *"Inno di Mameli,"* Mameli's Hymn.

Scipio refers to a commander, also known as Scipio Africano, who defended the Roman Republic and defeated the Carthaginian army in 202 B.C.E. *"Dell'elmo... s'e cinta la testa,"* literally means "with the helmet... is bound the head," figuratively, it means that Italy is armed. *"Le porga la chioma"* literally means "to-her (Italy) may-she (Victory)-give her hair. In ancient Rome female slaves wore short hair; Victory is called upon to give up her hair, too, as a sign that she will serve only Italy and not its enemies. *"Ché"* is short for *perché*. *"Schiava di Roma Iddio la creò"* means that God created Victory to serve as a slave to Rome, the ancient capital of Italy and, to Mameli, the future capital also.

Only the first part of the anthem is given here; it continues with a contrasting section and a repetition of the first 16 measures.

Quel mazzolin di fiori Track 56

Anonymous   **Anonymous, North Italian**

Quel maz - zo - lin_____ di fio - ri_____ che vien dal - la mon -
/kwel mat:tsolin di fjo:ri ke vjɛn dal:la montaɲa,/

ta - gna, quel maz - zo - lin_____ di fio - ri_____ che

vien dal - la mon - ta - gna, e guar-da ben che no'l se ba -
/e gwarda_ bɛn ke nol se baɲ:ɲa

gna che lo vo - glio re - ga - lar, e guar - da ben che no'l se
ke lo vɔʎ:ʎo regalar./

ba - gna ché lo vo - glio re - ga - lar._____

2. Lo voglio regalare,
   /lo vɔʎ:ʎo regala:re/
   perché l'è un bel mazzetto, (repeat first two lines)
   /perke lɛ un bɛl mat:tsɛt:to/
   lo voglio dare al mio moretto
   /lo vɔʎ:ʎo da:re al mio morɛt:to/
   questa sera quando'l vien. (repeat last two lines)
   /kwɛsta se:ra kwandol vjɛn/

1. That little bunch of flowers that comes from the mountains,
   watch out well that it doesn't get soaked, because I want to give it away.

2. I want to give it away because it is a pretty bouquet;
   I want to give it to my brown-haired boyfriend this evening when he comes.

   This song, about a girl who has picked flowers for her boyfriend, is a favorite of male choruses made up of *alpinisti*, men who climb the Italian Alps. After the freely sung opening solo lines, the rest of the song is sung vigorously, almost in march time.

Santa Lucia  Track 57

Teodoro Cottrau

Teodoro Cottrau

Andantino

Sul ma — re luc-ci-ca l'a-stro d'ar-gen — to, pla - ci - da è l'on — da, pro-spe-ro è il ven — to: Ve - ni-te al - l'a-gi-le bar-chet — ta mi — a, San - ta Lu - ci - a! San - ta Lu — ci — a! Ve - ni-te al - l'a-gi-le bar-chet — ta mi — a, San - ta Lu - ci - a! San - ta Lu - ci - a!

/sul ma:re lut:tʃika lastro dardʒɛnto plaːtʃida ɛ londa prɔspero ɛ il vɛnto/ /veniːte aliː laːdʒile barkɛtːta miːa santa lutʃiːa/

---

2. O dolce Napoli,
/o doltʃe naːpoli/
O suol beato,
/o swɔl beaːto/
Ove sorridere
/oːve sorːriːdere/
Volle il creato, (repeat first four lines)
/vɔlːle il kreaːto/

tu sei l'impero
/tu sɛi limpɛːro/
dell'armonia!
/delːlarmoniːa/
Santa Lucia!
Santa Lucia! (repeat last four lines)

1. Over the sea shines the silver star;
calm are the waves, favorable is the
wind. Come to the quick little boat of
mine: Santa Lucia! Santa Lucia!

2. O sweet Naples, o blessed ground,
where all creation wanted to smile,
you are the empire of harmony: Santa
Lucia! Santa Lucia!

In this song a boatman invites passengers to sail with him and calls out the name of his destination, *porto Santa Lucia*, a small marina located west of the busy main port of Naples. The area, famous for characteristic restaurants, is named after its parish church, St. Lucia's.

Although *"Santa Lucia"* is a song about Naples, the text is in standard Italian. The complete text had six stanzas. It was probably written by the composer, Teodoro Cottrau /teodoːro kɔtro/ (1827–1879), the son of a French musician.

Cottrau has been accused of stealing his most popular song from an unknown boatman, but his authorship seems to be satisfactorily documented. According to James J. Fuld's

The Book of World Famous Music (1971), the undated, probable first printing of *"Santa Lucia"* was in *Collezione completa delle canzoncine nazionali napoletane*. Both the first edition and the second (1865) affirm that Cottrau composed *"Santa Lucia"* on October 28, 1850, that is, before his 23rd birthday. He dedicated it to a Signorina Adolfina Deutz.

"Santa Lucia" has been re-printed hundreds of times, usually without the dotted rhythm in m2 and m4. This version conforms to the 1865 edition, published by Cottrau's own firm. The original key was E♭ Major.

Tu scendi dalle stelle

 Track 58

Alfonso Maria de' Liguori, 1755   **Alfonso Maria de' Liguori**

2. A te che sei del mondo il creatore,
   /a te ke sɛi del mondo il kreato:re/
   Mancano panni e fuoco, o mio Signore. (repeat)
   /maŋkano pan:ni e fwɔ:ko o mi:o siɲ:ɲo:re/
   Caro eletto Pargoletto,
   /ka:ro elet:to pargolet:to/
   Quanto questa povertà
   /kwanto kwesta poverta /
   Più m'innamora,
   /pju min:namo:ra/
   Giacché ti fece Amor povero ancora. (repeat)
   /dʒak:ke ti fe:tʃe amor pɔ:vero aŋko:ra/

1. You come from the stars, o King of Heaven, and come to a grotto,
   to cold and freezing. O my divine baby, I see you trembling here.
   O beloved God, and how much it cost you to have loved me!

2. To you, who are the Creator of the world, clothing and fire are
   lacking, o my Lord. Dear, chosen little boy, how much this poverty
   makes me fall in love with you, since Love made you poor again.

De' Liguori (1696–1787), a native of Naples, was a priest, an influential moral theologian and a creative poet and musician. He hoped to awaken religious devotion in the lower classes in southern Italy by means of his inspirational books and little songs, *canzoncine*. He created both texts and melodies, but he may have derived this melody from one written in 1738 by another composer, Monsignor Felice de' Paù. De' Liguori was canonized in 1837.

"*Tu scendi dalle stelle*" is by far the most popular Italian Christmas song. The 6/8 meter is associated with the music that is played by shepherds who visit the streets of southern Italian cities during the Christmas season.

Va, pensiero

Track 59

Temistocle Solera, 1842   **Giuseppe Verdi, 1842**

Va, pen - sie - ro,   sull'a - li   do - ra - te,   va ti
/va pensjɛːro   sulːlaːli   doraːte   va ti

po - sa   sui cli - vi,   sui col - li   o - ve o - lez - za - no te - pi - de e
pɔːza   sui kliːvi   sui kɔlːli   oːveoledːdzano   tɛːpideː

mol - li   l'au - re dol - ci   del suo - lo   na - tal!   Del Gior-
mɔlːli   laure doltʃi   del swɔːlo   nataːl   del dʒor-

da - no   le ri - ve sa - lu - ta,   di Si - on - ne   le tor - ri at - ter -
daːno   le riːve saluːta   di sionːne   le torːri atːterːraːte

ra - te   Oh mia pa - tria   sí bel - la e   per - du - ta,   Oh mem-
o   mia paːtrja   si bɛlːla e   perduːta   o mem-

bran - za sí ca - ra e fa - tal!   Ar - pa d'or dei fa - ti - di - ci
brantsa   si kaːra   e fataːl   arpa dɔr dei fatiːditʃi

va - ti,   per - ché mu - ta   dal sa - li - ce pen - di?   Le me-
vaːti   perke muːta   dal saːlitʃe   pɛndi   le me-

mo - rie nel pet - to rac - cen - di,   ci fa - vel - la   del tem - po che
mɔːrje nel pɛtto   rattʃɛndi   tʃi favɛlːla   del tɛmpo   ke

fu!   O si - mi - le   di So - li - ma a i fa - ti   trag - gi un
fu   o   sim iːle   di sɔːlimai   faːti   tradːdʒi un

suo   no   di cru - do   la - men - to.   O t'i - spi - ri il Si - gno re un con-
swɔːno   di kruːdo   lamɛnto   o   tispiːril   sino ːrɛ un   kon-

cen - to   che ne in-fon - da al pa - ti - re vir - tù   che ne in-fon - da al pa-
tʃɛnto   ke ne infɔndal   patiːre   virtuː   che ne in-fon - da al pa-

ti - - re vir - tú,   che ne in-fon - da al pa - ti - - re vir -

tù,   al pa - ti - re vir - tù!

Go, thoughts, on golden wings! Go, rest on the hills and mountains where the sweet breezes of my
native land freely and softly blow their fragrance. Greet the banks of the Jordan and the ruined
towers of Zion. Oh my homeland so beautiful and lost! Oh memory so dear and filled with death!

Golden harp of the prophet bards, why are you hanging silent on the willow tree?
Rekindle the memories in our hearts; tell us about the times that were!

Oh, like Jerusalem's fates you are bearing a sound of deep sorrow.
Oh, may the Lord inspire you with a harmony that instills in us the strength to endure!

Verdi's opera *Nabucco* is loosely based on a story from the Bible and is named for a Babylonian king who is known in English as Nebuchadnezzar. It concerns the destruction of Jerusalem in 586 B.C.E. and the captivity of the Jews in Babylon. The chorus of Jews sings *"Va, pensiero"* by the banks of the Euphrates River, sending their loving thoughts back to their desolated homeland.

When this opera was first sung in 1842, the audience made an immediate connection between the misery of the enchained Jews in Babylon and their own resentment against being ruled by Austria. Verdi's inspiring melody made him almost overnight into a hero of Italian patriotism. Because it depicts a state of victimization, *"Va, pensiero"* was not chosen to be the national anthem of the Italian Republic, but it is more beloved and more often sung than the chosen anthem, *"Fratelli d'Italia."*

In *Nabucco*, Act III, scene 4, this chorus has a long orchestral introduction. Verdi made the melody of *"Va, pensiero"* impressive by using unison voices; the chorus breaks into full harmony in m18. While singing, be attentive to the difference between the dotted rhythms in the chorus part and the prevailing triplets in the orchestra; they are intentionally independent from each other. When a slur marking connects two syllables, as in m2 and many places thereafter, there is a *portamento;* at the end of the first note value the voice, still singing the first syllable, changes to the second pitch, producing a quick grace note to the second note. The staccato markings in m10 and later are emotional in character, not light or happy. The original key is F# Major.

Neapolitan Songs

Two popular songs that the whole world associates with Italy are songs that must be sung in Neapolitan, rather than standard Italian. Neapolitan uses many words that are not Italian, and words that are common to both may be pronounced quite differently. The most striking difference is that Neapolitan uses a neutral vowel, or schwa /ə/, which is unknown in Italian. Also closed and open E and O are used differently in Neapolitan than in Italian.

An article by Arthur Graham, *"Singing the Neapolitan Song"* (*The NATS Bulletin*, March/April 1984), contains general information and phonetic information about several Neapolitan songs. A Neapolitan actor, Claudio Giova, generously provided specific information about these two songs.

Funiculí-funiculà   Track 60

Giuseppe Turco   **Luigi Denza, 1880**

'ncop - pa, jam - mo   ja,_____   Jam - mo   jam - mo   'ncop - pa, jam - mo
nkɔpːpə jamːmə   ja

ja,   Fu - ni - cu - lí,   fu - ni - cu - là,   fu - ni - cu - lí,   fu - ni - cu - là!
funikuli   funikula/

'Ncop - pa, jam - mo   ja,   fu - ni - cu - lí,   fu - ni - cu - là!

Stanza 1:

Italian translation:

Ieri sera, ohimè, io sono salito—
    tu sai a dove?
A dove questo core ingrato piú dispetto
    non puó farmi!
A dove il fuoco cuoce, ma se fuggi,
    ti lascia stare!
E non ti corre appresso, non ti strugge,
    in cielo guardare!
Andiamo, andiamo sopra, andiamo,
    Funiculí, funiculà!

English translation:

Yesterday evening, oh! I got on board—
    you know to where?
To where this ungrateful heart cannot do
    more cruelty to me!
To where the fire cooks, but if you run away,
    it lets you alone!
And does not run after you, torment you,
    looking at the sky!
Let's go up, let's go,
    Funiculí, funiculà!

Stanza 2:

Neapolitan: Ne'... jammo da la terra a la   muntagna!
IPA: /nɛ jamːmə da la tɛrːra la muntanːɲa/
Italian: Dunque, andiamo de la terra a la montagna!
English: So, let's go from the lowland to the mountain!

  no passo nc'e'!
  /nu pasːsontʃɛ/
  Non c'è un passo!
  There's not a step to take!

  Se vede Francia, Proceta e la Spagna...
  /sə veːdə frantʃa prɔːtʃətɛ la spanːɲa/
  Si vedono la Francia, Procida e la Spagna…
  One sees France, Procida and Spain—

  Io veco a tte!
  /io veːka tːte/
  io ti vedo!
  I look at you!

Tirato co la fune, ditto'n fatto,
/tiraːtə kɔ la fuːnə dɪtːtən fatːtə/
Tirato con la fune, detto è fatto,
Pulled by the rope, no sooner said than done,

  'Ncielo se va!
  /ntʃeːlə sə va/
  in cielo si va!
  to the sky one goes!

  Se va comm' 'a lu viento a l'intrasatto,
  /sə va kɔmːma lu vjɛnta lintrasatːtə/
  Si va come il vento all'improvviso,
  One goes like the wind all of a sudden,

  gue', saglie, sa!
  /we saʎːʎə sa/
  ehi, salga, salga!
  so, climb on, climb on!

In 1880 a funicular (a railroad pulled by a cable) was opened to carry sightseers up the side of Mt. Vesuvius near Naples. A contest was conducted for the best song to celebrate the achievement, and this song took the first prize.

Giuseppe Turco, the poet, was a journalist. Luigi Denza (Castellammare di Stabia, 1846–London, 1922) studied composition under Mercadante at the Naples conservatory. Later in life, he settled in London, where he became the director of the London Academy of Music and later a professor of singing at the Royal Academy of Music. He composed over 500 vocal works. "Funiculí, funiculà" was quoted in orchestra works by Nicolai Rimsky-Korsakov and Richard Strauss as if it were an anonymous folksong.

The meaningless syllables *funiculí-funiculà* merely play with the sounds in the word *funiculare*. Notice that the first word of the song loses its final vowel because the next word begins with a vowel; this happens often in Neapolitan. *Oi' ne'* resembles Italian *oimè* (alas), but the meaning varies with the inflection and can be happy. *Jammo ja* and *saglie sa* are particularly Neapolitan expressions: instead of a word being repeated, only the first syllable is repeated. *Muntagna* would normally end with /ə/, but in this case it rhymes with *Spagna*. *Proceta* (Procida) is an island 21 km out in the Mediterranean Sea from Naples.

'O sole mio

Giovanni Capurro

Eduardo Di Capua, 1898

Andantino

Che bel - la co - sa è 'na jur - na - ta 'e so - le,____
kə bɛl:la kɔ:zɛ na jurna:te so:lə

____ n'a - ria se - re - na dop - - - po na tem - pe - sta!____
narja sərɛːnə dɔp:pə na təmpɛstə

____ Pe' ll'a - ria fre - sca pa - re già na fe - sta...____
pəl:larja frɛʃkə paːrə diːdʒa na fɛstə

____ Che bel - la co - sa è 'na jur - na - ta 'e so - le.

____ Ma n'a - tu so - le____ cchiù bel - lo, oi - ne',____
ma na tu so:lə kju bɛl:lɔi ne

____ 'o so - le mi - o,____ sta nfron - te a te!____
o so:lə mi:ə stanfrɔnta te

'o so - - - - le, 'o so - le mi - o,
o so:loso:lə mi:ə

sta nfron - te a te,_____ sta nfron - te a te!_____

Stanza 1:

Singable Italian translation:
Che bella cosa è una giornata di sole,
un'aria serena dopo una tempesta!
Per l'aria fresca pare già una festa...
Ma c'hai tu sole piú bello, ohimè,
Il sole mio sta nella fronte tua.

English translation:
What a beautiful thing is a day of sunshine,
clear air after a storm!
The fresh air already makes it seem a festival...
But you have sun more beautiful, indeed,
my sun is in your face!

Stanza 2:

Neapolitan: Lúcene e llastre d''a fenesta toia;
IPA: /lu:tʃəne l:lastrə da fənɛsta to:jə/
Italian: Risplendono i vetri della fenestra tua;
English: The panes of your window shine;

'na lavannare canta e se ne vanta,
/na lavan:na:rə kantɛ sə nə vantə/
una lavandaia canta e se ne vanta...
a laundrywoman sings and is proud of it...

e pe' tramente torce, spanne e canta, Lúcene, etc.
/e pə tramɛntə tɔrtʃə ʃpan:nə kantə/
e nel frattempo lei torce, stende e canta,...
and meanwhile she wrings the laundry, spreads it
out and sings,

Stanza 3.

Quanno fa notte e 'o sole se ne scenne,
/kwan:nə fa nɔt:te o so:lə sə nə ʃen:nə/
Quando fa notte e il sole scende,
When it is night and the sun goes down,

mme vene quase 'na malincunia;
/mə vɛ:nə kwa:sə na malinkuni:ə/
A me viene quasi una malinconia;
to me comes almost a melancholy.

sotto 'a fenesta toia restarria. Quanno, etc.
/sot:ta fənɛsta to:ja rəstar:riə/
sotto la fenestra tua resterei
under your window I would like to stay.

The poet, Giovanni Capurro (1859–1920), was born and died in Naples. The same was true of Eduardo di Capua (1864–1917), who graduated from the conservatory and earned his living playing in cafes and small theaters and, later, in cinemas. He sold his songs outright, and despite their great success he died in extreme poverty. *'O sole mio* (dedicated to Tomasino Rebolla) won a competition in 1898 and was published the next year. Many editions give incorrect words, but this text has been verified with the first edition that was published for export in 1901 by the original publisher, Bideri, Naples.

'O stands for *lo* (the), not for the exclamation "oh."

Bibliography

The most important reference works on Italian phonetics are:

Canepàri, Luciano. *Dizionario di pronuncia italiana.* Bologna: Zanichelli, 1999. Known as *il DiPI.* Pronunciations only, no meanings, detailed, including proper names.

Canepàri, Luciano. *Manuale di pronuncia italiana.* Bologna: Zanichelli, 1999. Known as *il MaPI.* Scientific study of every aspect of Italian speech, standard and dialect.

Several fine dictionaries are published in Italy; the one used as an authority for this book was:

Zingarelli, Nicola. *Vocabolario della lingua italiana.* Bologna: Zanichelli, 1989, 11th edition. The only full-sized Italian dictionary with IPA (transcriptions by Piero Fiorelli and Ilio Calabresi). Excellent for verb forms and for obsolete and literary words. (The 12th edition does not have IPA.)

The following books have also been useful in preparing this book:

Adams, David. *A Handbook of Diction for Singers: Italian, German, French.* New York: Oxford University Press, 1999.

Blankenburg, Heinz. *Italian Pronunciation for Singers.* Privately printed.

Carta, Mario. *Italian for Singers.* Unpublished.

Coffin, Berton, Ralph Errolle and others. *Phonetic Readings of Songs and Arias.* Metuchen, NJ: Scarecrow, rev. 1982. IPA transcriptions of standard repertoire in Italian, French and German.

Colorni, Evelina. *Singer's Manual of Italian Diction.* New York: G. Schirmer, 1970.

Errolle, Ralph. *Italian Diction for Singers.* Boulder, CO: Pruett Press, 1963.

Handbook of the International Phonetic Association: a guide to the use of the International Phonetic Alphabet. Cambridge: Cambridge University Press, 1999.

Lanarni, Ughetta. *Manuale di dizione e pronuncia.* Firenze: Giunti, 1999.

Migliorini, Bruno, Carlo Tagliavini and Piero Fiorelli. *Dizionario d'ortografia e di pronuncia.* Torino: Radiotelevisione Italiana (RAI), 1969, second edition.

Pullum, Geoffrey K., and William A. Ladusaw. *Phonetic Symbol Guide.* Chicago: University of Chicago Press, 1996, 2nd edition.

Although these sources do not deal with diction, they are useful sources of translations and language information:

Berrong, Richard M. *Grammar and Translation for the Italian Libretto.* New York: Excalibur, 1996. Hundreds of examples of word usage and translation knots untied.

Bleiler, Ellen. (141) *Famous Italian Opera Arias.* Mineola, NY: Dover Publications, 1996.

Ezust, Emily. Lied and Song Texts Page. www.recmusic.org/lieder.

Gallotta, Bruno. *Manuale di poesia e musica.* Milano: Rugginenti Editore, 2001.

Lakeway, Ruth, and Robert C. White, Jr. *Italian Art Song.* Bloomington, IN: Indiana University Press, 1989.

LeVan, Timothy. *Masters of the Italian Art Song.* Metuchen: Scarecrow, 1990.

Schoep, Arthur, and Daniel Harris, *Word-by-Word Translations of Songs and Arias, Part II — Italian.* Metuchen: Scarecrow, 1972.

All volumes of the Alfred Vocal Masterworks Series contain both IPA and word-by-word translations, including these titles:

Gateway to Italian Art Songs

26 *Italian Songs and Arias*

(26) *Italian Arias of the Baroque and Classic Eras*

(14) *Italian Art Songs of the Romantic Era*

20 *Songs by Donizetti*

Songs and Duets of Garcia, Malibran and Viardot

Index

Words shown in SMALL CAPITALS are defined on the first page listed.
Poets and composers of the songs on pages 106–115 are not indexed.

The International Phonetic Alphabet (revised to 1993)

Consonants (Pulmonic)

	Bilabial	Labiodental	Dental	Alveolar	Postalveolar	Retroflex	Palatal	Velar	Uvular	Pharyngeal	Glottal
Plosive	p b			t d		ʈ ɖ	c ɟ	k g	q ɢ		ʔ
Nasal	m	ɱ		n		ɳ	ɲ	ŋ	N		
Trill	B			r					R		
Tap or Flap				ɾ		ɽ					
Fricative	ɸ β	f v	θ ð	s z	ʃ ʒ	ʂ ʐ	ç ʝ	x ɣ	χ ʁ	ħ ʕ	h ɦ
Lateral fricative				ɬ ɮ							
Approximant		ʋ		ɹ		ɻ	j	ɰ			
Lateral approximant				l		ɭ	ʎ	L			

Where symbols appear in pairs, the one to the right represents a voiced consonant. Shaded areas denote articulations judged impossible.

Consonants (Non-Pulmonic)

Clicks		Voiced implosives		Ejectives	
ʘ	Bilabial	ɓ	Bilabial	ʼ	as in:
ǀ	Dental	ɗ	Dental/alveolar	pʼ	Bilabial
ǃ	(Post)alveolar	ʄ	Palatal	tʼ	Dental/alveolar
ǂ	Palatoalveolar	ɠ	Velar	kʼ	Velar
ǁ	Alveolar lateral	ʛ	Uvular	sʼ	Alveolar fricatve

Vowels

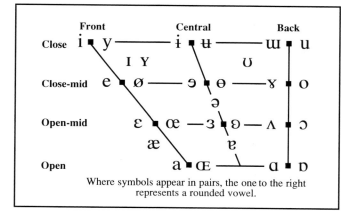

Where symbols appear in pairs, the one to the right represents a rounded vowel.

Other Symbols

ʍ Voiceless labial-velar fricative	ɕ ʑ Alveolo-palatal fricatives
w Voiced labial-velar approximant	ɺ Alveolar lateral flap
ɥ Voiced labial-palatal approximant	ɧ Simultaneous ʃ and x
ʜ Voiceless epiglottal fricative	
ʢ Voiced epiglottal fricative	Affricates and double articulations can be represented by two symbols joined by a tie bar, if necessary
ʡ Epiglottal plosive	k͡p t͡s

Suprasegmentals

ˈ	Primary stress	ˌfoʊnəˈtɪʃən
ˌ	Secondary stress	
ː	Long	eː
ˑ	Half-long	eˑ
˘	Extra-short	ĕ
.	Syllable break	ɹi.ækt
|	Minor (foot) group	
‖	Major (intonation) group	
‿	Linking (absence of a break)	

TONES & WORD ACCENTS

LEVEL		CONTOUR	
e̋ or ˥	Extra high	ě or ˩˥	Rising
é ˦	High	ê ˥˩	Falling
ē ˧	Mid	e̋ ˦˥	High rising
è ˨	Low	e̥ ˩˨	Low rising
ȅ ˩	Extra low	ẽ ˧˦˧	Rising-falling etc.
↓ Downstep		↗ Global rise	
↑ Upstep		↘ Global fall	

Diacritics

Diacritics may be placed above a symbol with a descender, e.g.: ŋ̊

̥	Voiceless	n̥ d̥	̤	Breathy voiced	b̤ a̤	̪	Dental	t̪ d̪
̬	Voiced	s̬ t̬	̰	Creaky voiced	b̰ a̰	̺	Apical	t̺ d̺
ʰ	Aspirated	tʰ dʰ	̼	Linguolabial	t̼ d̼	̻	Laminal	t̻ d̻
̹	More rounded	ɔ̹	ʷ	Labialized	tʷ dʷ	̃	Nasalized	ẽ
̜	Less rounded	ɔ̜	ʲ	Palatized	tʲ dʲ	ⁿ	Nasal release	dⁿ
̟	Advanced	u̟	ˠ	Velarized	tˠ dˠ	ˡ	Lateral release	dˡ
̠	Retracted	i̠	ˤ	Pharyngealized	tˤ dˤ	̚	No audible release	d̚
̈	Centralized	ë	̴	Velarized or pharyngealized	ɫ		
̽	Mid-centralized	ě	̝	Raised	e̝ (ɹ̝ =voiced alveolar fricative)		
̩	Syllabic	l̩	̞	Lowered	e̞ (β̞ =voiced bilabial approximant)		
̯	Non-syllabic	e̯	̘	Advanced Tongue Root	e̘		
˞	Rhoticity	ɚ	̙	Retracted Tongue Root	e̙		

Phonemes of Italian

IPA Symbols	Symbol Names	Similar English Sounds	Page
1. [i]	Lower-case I	mach<u>i</u>ne	32
2. [e]	Lower-case E	ch<u>a</u>otic	34
3. [ɛ]	Epsilon	r<u>e</u>d	35
4. [a]	Lower-case A	<u>ai</u>sle	37
5. [u]	Lower-case U	tr<u>u</u>th	38
6. [o]	Lower-case O	<u>o</u>ceanic	39
7. [ɔ]	Open O	<u>ou</u>ght	40
8. [j]	Lower-case J	<u>y</u>es	42
9. [w]	Lower-case W	<u>w</u>et	43
10. [m]	Lower-case M	<u>m</u>ime	50
11. [n]	Lower-case N	<u>n</u>oon	51
12. [ɲ]	Left-tail N	(none in English)	52
13. [ŋ]	Eng	si<u>ng</u>	53
14. [l]	Lower-case L	<u>l</u>augh	54
15. [ʎ]	Turned Y	(none in English)	55
16. [r] or [ɾ]	Lower-case R Fishhook R	(trill R, none in English) me<u>rr</u>y (formal, tap R)	56
17. [p]	Lower-case P	<u>p</u>ie	59
18. [b]	Lower-case B	<u>b</u>uy	60
19. [t]	Lower-case T	<u>t</u>oo	61
20. [d]	Lower-case D	<u>d</u>o	62
21. [k]	Lower-case K	<u>c</u>ap	63
22. [g]	Lower-case G	<u>g</u>ap	64
23. [f]	Lower-case F	<u>f</u>at	65
24. [v]	Lower-case V	<u>v</u>at	66
25. [s]	Lower-case S	<u>S</u>ue	67
26. [z]	Lower-case Z	<u>z</u>oo	68
27. [ʃ]	Esh	<u>sh</u>oe	69
28. [ts]	T-S affricate	si<u>ts</u> up	70
29. [dz]	D-Z affricate	a<u>dds</u> on	71
30. [tʃ]	T-Esh affricate	<u>ch</u>urch	72
31. [dʒ]	D-Yogh affricate	<u>j</u>udge	73